ADIRONTREKS

PLACES AND PEOPLE IN THE ADIRONDACKS

JOHN VESTY

A CROSSROADS PUBLICATION

ISBN 0-9626876-0-X
Library of Congress Catalog Card Number: 90-82523

A Crossroads Publication of
John Vesty Company
Box 244
Indian Lake, NY 12842

To all
who call
the Adirondacks
home

*"The Moving Finger writes; and, having
writ,
Moves on:—"*
Omar Khayyám

     As much as any map, the words of others have charted the course of these travels. I am indebted to all who have preserved their account of the Adirondacks, including:

Ted Aber and Stella King for "The History of Hamilton County";
Alfred L. Donaldson for "A History of the Adirondacks,"
volumes 1 and 2;

Barney Fowler for "Adirondack Album," volumes 1, 2 and 3;

Frank Graham, Jr. for "The Adirondack Park: A Political History";

Larry Hart for "The Sacandaga Story, A Valley of Yesteryear";

Henry Harter for "Fairy Tale Railroad";

Harvey Kaiser for "Great Camps of the Adirondacks";

T. Morris Longstreth for "The Adirondacks";

Barbara McMartin for "Discover the Adirondacks, 1";

Roger Trancik for "Hamlets of the Adirondacks";

William Chapman White for "Just About Everything in the Adirondacks."

Too, I would like to thank Alice and Craig Gilborn of the Adirondack Museum for their suggestions, the Essex County Historical Society and the Boquet River Association for background information about the communities of Essex County, and my wife Pauletta for her steadfast support throughout the project. Were it not for her encouragement, this moving finger would yet be stalled somewhere between rough notes and first draft. I am especially grateful to all the people I encountered in the course of my travels. ADIRONTREKS is their story.

Roadside sign at Hadley

CONTENTS

Blazing
the Trail

WHO would think a few words with a stranger in a checkout line could lead to a book?

"Guess Iowa's no place to live," said the man behind me, pointing to a headline at the tabloid rack. UFO aliens, it seems, were holding a town in Iowa hostage.

"Hope they don't try that in the Adirondacks," I replied, "…unless they'd take some scenery for ransom."

"Ohhh…good country up there! Used to go to Loon Lake every summer."

"Sure…over by Chestertown." I spoke like an authority. After all, Loon Lake wasn't far from where we were moving.

"Chestertown?" questioned the man. "Don't recall that place."

Of course, we were speaking of different Loon Lakes—one in the eastern Adirondacks, the other far to the north…yet both well within the six million-acre Adirondack Park. When you're dissecting an area the size of Massachusetts it's easy to confuse places, especially places with the same name.

I had heard of people moving to a new area without knowing much about it. That's not going to happen to us, I would say. After all, our family had been coming to the Adirondacks for over 20 years. The mountains held no surprises for us—or so I thought. Now on the verge of packing up, I started to wonder.

The stranger's face soon faded from memory, but not our conversation. Returning home, I pulled out an Esso map of the state which dated from the era when gas stations gave them away. Roads don't change much once you get away from the city.

Sure enough, there was the other Loon Lake—plus a vast expanse north of Saranac Lake I had never seen. Good hunting country, I had been told. Perhaps so, but people also live in places like Owls Head, Mountain View, Santa Clara. There was even another Indian Lake—still in the Park, too. Here I had been coming to Indian Lake all these years without realizing there was a namesake to the north.

Come to think of it, my acquaintance with the Adirondacks was largely limited to the narrow strip along Route 8 as far as Speculator, then north on Route 30. Those were our roads to the woods—each camp along the way a neighbor, each bump an old friend. The trip brought few surprises. Looking back I now realize this was the extent of my Adirondack expertise—just two roads.

Out of curiosity, I counted the places I had visited within the Blue Line, as the Park boundary is called. This took only a minute, for I was a stranger to all but a few. Then and there, I vowed to learn more of the area we were about to call home....to search out every place from Bellmont Center to Bleecker, from Number Four to Essex—wherever people lived in the Park. That was over four years and 200 places ago.

The Esso map brought "Happy Motoring" as far as Warren County. Here I lost my way on a back road in search of Thurman, to which the map had assigned a dot. Thurman, it turned out, is not a dot, but a township of considerable size. I still recall that day in the middle of Thurman, asking the people in a garage how to get where I already was. They had fun giving me directions.

At least I was not alone in my ignorance. Other maps had made the same mistake. That's one of the troubles with maps. An error is often repeated. But a town by any other designation is still a town. Occasionally a map retains the name of a place which no longer exists. This often happens in the mountains where an empty space is just waiting to be filled. Mapmakers should seek out some of the places they've listed.

They'd be surprised when they start looking for names like Oregon and Griffin along Route 8. I know little of Oregon other than it once had a tannery. Griffin was quite a community at the turn of the century, I understand. Now both are gone and the Siamese Ponds Wilderness Area pushes against the road. Still, Oregon and Griffin are remembered on some of the maps. So are other names from the past. Separating yesterday from today can sometimes be a problem.

Obviously, I needed a map of the region which was both accurate and detailed—one which would direct me around hills and backroads, and get me home again. A few weeks after the Thurman episode, my search for improved charting was rewarded when I came upon a folding map in a diner.

Finally I had found what every newcomer needs—a map showing all the roads, town boundaries, every place people might live. Naturally, a chart of such detail is large. But then, how often would you navigate a narrow road while unfolding a map to the dimensions of a small bedsheet? Just once...then you learn to crease it to manageable size before driving off.

By the end of my journey, the map was in shreds from constant folding and unfolding. Highways located at a crease were now but a tear. I tell friends such roads are under construction. Some have offered to replace my abused map, but I respectfully decline. It has served me well, and I shall keep it, tears and all, as a memento of these treks through the mountains.

Before embarking, I knew nothing of Sugar Bush, Alder Brook, Franklin Falls, Hawkeye. I still know but little of these—or many other places I visited. The difference between nothing and little is what this book is about.

My new map was good, but not perfect. I found a road marker for Sugar Bush along Route 3 at the same intersection the map had located Merrills Corners. Somehow I feel the state sign crew was correct. Down the road I came to Alder Brook, unmarked and unnamed on the map. Yet there it was, complete with a hand-lettered sign and cemetery. Alder

Brook was signed, sealed, and delivered—despite what the map said.

The stage used to stop at Franklin Falls on its way over from Ausable Forks. Yet I found nothing along the crumbling road. Now the map was even with me. It had not listed Franklin Falls. It did list Hawkeye, however. But I found only a long-established cabin resort along the shores of Silver Lake. Sometimes even a detailed map doesn't work. It takes a native to blaze some trails. Maybe that's the way it should be.

My questions mounted with the miles. Why would an intersection with nothing but a cornfield be called Lord Corners? Was a church once here, or perhaps a family named Lord? Someone recalled a grocery store at the intersection. Lord knows what was there, not I. On and on I could go—ten questions for each answer. But then, I do not profess this to be a textbook.

At first, I was concerned what to call these places in the woods. Are they towns, villages, hamlets—what have you? Then I listened to the people who live here.

"I'm going into town," a person might say.

"OK...I'll see you in the village then," comes a ready answer.

Everyone understands "town" and "village" even when the reference is to a hamlet. But how often do you hear a person say: "Are you going to the hamlet?" Somehow, "hamlet" just doesn't translate to conversation. It's better left as a road marker or a zoning classification.

People don't talk much about settlements, either. "Oh, you mean a little place," they might say—and indeed it is. In fact, "little places" are often on the edge of extinction, a family or two from nothing. If a settlement happens to have "Mill" in its name, there's a good chance it already is a nonplace…a term I use not to make light its history, but rather to show present status.

Several "Corners" are now but brush or field. "Junctions" and "Stations" went the way of the railroad, though a crumbling station house might still be seen. Names linger long after a settlement fades. Like Dorothy in the Land of Oz, it's easy to lose one's way in search of a fanciful nonplace along an unnamed road.

During my travels I came upon a man living at the western edge of the Park who told of walking to Perkins Clearing north of Speculator for a few days of fishing. By road, the trip might be a hundred miles.

"You walked a hundred miles to go fishing?" I asked.

"No…more like fifty."

Later I checked the map and sure enough—a hike along the Moose River and across Moose River Plains was about fifty miles. So I had learned something more of the Adirondacks: the shortest distance between two places is probably by trail—not highway. Of course, any kid who's taken a shortcut to school might have told me as much. But after a lifetime of asphalt and concrete it's easy to forget about shortcuts.

Adirondack roadways skirt wilderness and mountains, stretching the distance between places. On a clear day you can see Marcy and the High Peaks from the hilltop at Indian Lake—a distance of about 28 miles. A drive to the trailhead parking area at Upper Works is much longer... with Marcy still miles beyond.

Naturally, no one shortcut crosses six million acres. That's a lot of territory any way you slice it. The winding network of mountain roads only make it appear larger. Anyone in Inlet can tell you how long it takes to reach their county seat at Lake Pleasant. Quite a haul. In fact, you might start the morning in Stratford, on the southwest edge of the Park, and travel much of the day before arriving at Ellenburg Center to the north. I suspect not many living in one know of the other.

But travel the winding roads from place to place, season to season. Gradually, the miles and mountains fade, and physical differences disappear as a mosaic of Adirondack living emerges...a pattern of comfortable routines, predictable viewpoints, conservative values, independent life-styles. Adirondack towns share more than a common location within the largest park in the lower forty-eight.

Every community has a place like The Coffee Pot or Bill's Grocery where people can spend a little time talking about the weather or what's wrong with the car. Conversation is mostly nonnews—things you don't read in the weekly paper. That's just as well.

"Has Emma made it out of the house yet?" someone inquires. Everyone wants to know how she's doing after the operation.

"Who was the trooper chasing down your road last night?" asks another.

"You know," comes the sly reply. "And guess who was in the car with him!" Now everyone listens. This might just be the bulletin of the day.

Sometimes you hear about life at the edge of the forest.

"Finally figured out how to keep deer out of my garden."

"How's that?" you ask.

"Don't plant it!" Everyone at the counter laughs—sipping the morning's third cup of coffee.

People have fun in small towns. They don't mind a joke on themselves, or their neighbors. And you can tell a good story over and over. Like store cheese, it only improves with age.

Just about every town has a bulletin board where you can tack up a notice. There's always a CAR FOR SALE and it RUNS GOOD. Usually there's FIREWOOD FOR SALE, and a GARAGE SALE that's coming,

RAIN OR SHINE. In larger places, people look over the classifieds. In small towns, they check the bulletin board.

Imagine a town without a fire department! Who'd run the fairs and barbeques, or sound the noon whistle? Come to think of it, who else could put out the fires and help with emergencies? The fire department is at the core of village life. Most places could easier survive without a supervisor.

Small town churches are for more than worship, weddings and funerals. Often they're the center of social activity, too—for suppers and breakfasts, bake sales and bazaars, meetings and special events. They serve all the community.

People tend to get along with each other in a small town. One might not agree with another's viewpoint or lifestyle—yet it is tolerated. Together, the two might work on a community project, or help one another when needed. Family bonding is especially strong. If a mother works, a relative often cares for her children. I've seen a house built from foundation to roof by uncles and cousins—as plumb as any around.

Small town people tell it as it is—pure and simple. Frequently, newcomers are surprised when they first hear straight talk. How un-diplomatic, they think. But soon they discover the advantages of saying what they mean. Makes life easier.

Kids enjoy the good life of the mountains. Where else might they find lakes and wilderness in the backyard—snowmobiles and bikes in the frontyard? Kids are always on machines. So are their dads. Surely there's more going on in the city for kids. But that doesn't make life better. Town kids are not afraid to smile at a strange face—which says something about growing up in a small place.

Every town wears its history proudly. Old-timers speak firsthand of logging and river runs, of unpaved roads and old hotels, working the mines and farms now gone. Young people listen carefully.

"I wish someone would go to her house with a tape recorder, before it's too late." Over and over, you hear words like these. People want to preserve their history.

For much of the Adirondacks, yesterday was better. You see a community's past etched on its buildings—an empty grange hall, vacant stores, decaying barns. Quickly you realize this once was a farm center—a place to buy supplies and groceries, and sell the products of the land. Perhaps the town also had a gristmill, or a sawmill. Now they're gone, as are the farms—replaced by overgrown fields and memories.

Much the same has happened to the mining towns, the logging centers and milltowns which once prospered next to swift mountain streams. People have a way of hanging on long after a community falters.

After all, this is home. But walk the streets in search of new houses, new stores and shops. You won't find them. Most Adirondack towns show their age. With few exceptions, those doing well must thank the tourists for their good fortune. The others live in the past.

Here and there the Adirondack economy is robust. Places like Saranac Lake, Lake Placid and Lake George are doing quite well. Some others are holding their own, or growing slightly. No doubt that's a healthy sign, too. Yet much of the Park is in limbo. One can only wonder if there's enough tourism for all? Or if the tourists want what they see in some places. Time will tell.

Meanwhile, life goes on. The old grow older and so do their houses. The kids grow up and so do their machines—cars replacing bikes. Then one day they're taller than their parents, and out of high school— getting married and leaving town. They grow and go....because there's nothing else to do, no way out if they stick around. But it was a great place to be a kid. This is the reality of life in the woods.

For some, the limited opportunity of the mountains is enough—a job in the summer at the state park, waiting table, or for the lucky, a full-time job working for the town or state. Unfortunately, there aren't enough jobs to go around. How ironic—to taste Eden, then leave it to search for a better life. Surely they return to visit...proud in uniforms, talking about far-off places they never heard of before leaving home, driving new cars and looking prosperous, exuding city life—wishing they were home again. But once they've gone, things are never the same.

Those who stay to find seasonal work hope to qualify for "unenjoyment," as they might say—making light of their plight. The "off-season" in the mountains is long, unforgiving of those without steady work. So you do what you can—plowing driveways, a little carpentry or painting, cutting pulp and firewood, picking up odd jobs—whatever it takes to keep body and family together. Maybe those who came before had more job security—working the mine or papermill, running a farm.

Times have changed. Now the Park is protected like never before. Things are looking up for the woods—if not the woodsmen and woodswomen. But you don't talk about this at The Coffee Pot. It's just the feeling you get going from one town to another, seeing places and things as they are.

Then one day you start wondering: Who's out there carrying the banner for the towns which have lost their industry without finding tourism? Who's helping those sentenced to a lifetime of odd jobs and unemployment? Will the day come when the young can find steady work without leaving town? Right now there's more lobbying for Adirondack trees than Adirondack people. Are not the people of the woods as deserving as its pine and balsam? Some fear it's their turn to be clear-cut. Add Adirondack Man/Woman to the endangered list.

Enough of this bumpy political highway. Mine is a surer route, a tranquil journey of back roads where people yet celebrate the freedom and hardship of mountain life. Each day I have recorded as seen—a snapshot of that moment. Yet sometimes a snapshot is slightly out-of-focus, or even out-of-date before it reaches the family album. What follows is no exception. Seldom are first impressions perfect. At least I stopped to walk the streets—to watch and listen.

For that, I am less the stranger to Ironville, Wadhams, Reber, Standish, Jerusalem, Riparius—wherever these winding roads lead.

15

1

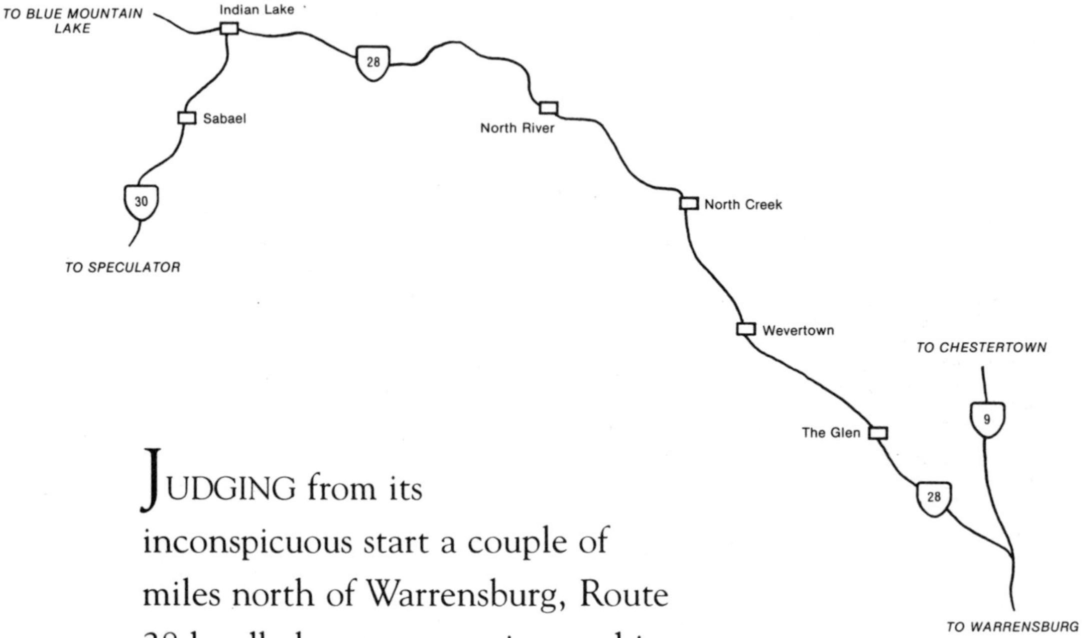

TO BLUE MOUNTAIN LAKE
Indian Lake
28
Sabael
30
TO SPECULATOR
North River
North Creek
Wevertown
TO CHESTERTOWN
The Glen
9
28
TO WARRENSBURG

THE GLEN
WEVERTOWN
NORTH CREEK
NORTH RIVER
INDIAN LAKE
SABAEL

JUDGING from its inconspicuous start a couple of miles north of Warrensburg, Route 28 hardly looms as a major road into the woods. Visiting motorists might expect this intersection to have more—perhaps a "Gateway to the Adirondacks" sign or a caution light. It has neither.

16

Not that it matters this midwinter day. The skiers have been to Gore Mountain before, and the UPS delivery truck makes the trip daily to North Creek and Indian Lake. Surely the loaded pulp truck can find its way to the papermill in Glens Falls. Such is January's limited commerce.

Soon the road crosses a depression carved by the Hudson River. This area is called The Glen, though The Gorge might better describe its location. Pioneer photographer Matthew Brady is said to have been born nearby. Many years ago, The Glen briefly had been the northern terminus of the rail line from Saratoga. But as soon as the remaining track had been laid to North Creek, The Glen became little more than a blur to passing trains.

Today, neither owner nor guest is in evidence at The Glen House. In the yard is the outline of a car—no doubt looking better in its blanket of snow than when spring arrives. Across the road a sign promotes whitewater rafting. But these riverside buildings also appear unoccupied. One might guess The Glen, momentarily at least, has a resident population of zero.

Now the radio voice grows weaker. Some people claim the iron deposits in the mountains soak up the radio waves. But WGY's 50,000 watts plows through the static all the way from Schenectady. More snow is coming tonight, I am told.

17

"But just an inch or two. And remember…all systems are GO for the new Grand Union opening…POP…SNAP…CRACKLE."

Even WGY has a tough time getting through today.

Wevertown has no "a" in its name. In fact, it has nothing to do with the weaving industry—not these days at least—though Mill Creek and Mill Mountain are here. A different story is told of how the place was named. Pioneer John Thurman, it seems, offered to name this new wilderness community for the first family to settle here. (He already had named Thurman and Johnsburg for himself, enough for one man.) Several families set forth on the difficult journey, but the Wever family was the first to reach this piece of Thurman's "promised land."

Wevertown has a lumberyard of considerable size, a real estate firm, UPS pickup, a gasoline/convenience store, and a municipal building with an empty sheriff's car parked alongside—a visual reminder that speeders along this section of Route 28 are taking their chances. At the foot of the hill is an attractive former church called "Mill Mountain."

Further along is a roadside diner with a big plastic Santa on the porch, and decorations for Valentine's Day inside. "BE MY VALENTINE" says the streamer above the coffee mugs. Small cutout hearts cover the walls, and a large heart-shaped balloon hangs from the ceiling in the adjoining dining room.

18

"Bet you'd never guess I like holidays," smiled the waitress.

"Wish I could take a holiday from this flu bug," said the bearded guy, hacking as he lit a fresh cigarette.

"Hear ninety kids are outa school in North Creek," replied the waitress, joining in with some hacking of her own.

Many a motorist bypasses North Creek, assuming the Ski Barn, condos and few other buildings visible from the highway is the extent of town. Actually, the structures seen on the north side of the road are in Holcombville, though hardly anyone makes that distinction these days. Further along is the Senior Center and the Tri-County Nursing Home. North Creek's lively business district lies just off the highway—complete with bank, restaurants, Grand Union, a printer which also publishes North Creek's own paper, the NEWS-ENTERPRISE—and several stores including Mountain Drugs and Sundries. Spectacular views of the surrounding mountains are everywhere.

At the outskirt of town is North Creek's Ski Bowl, one of the first ski centers in the state. But today the Bowl is dwarfed by the huge state-run facility on the other side of Gore Mountain operated by the Olympic Regional Development Authority.

On winter weekends, Gore's large parking lot is frequently packed—its slopes and lodge a beehive of activity. Gore Mountain has

changed the face of North Creek and surrounding area. Its economic impact is felt as far away as Lake George, 30 miles to the east. Today, 40 trails, all lifts, and the gondola are operating—with no waiting. By midmorning the parking lot starts to fill, though buses from New York won't arrive until tomorrow.

Years ago, skiers frequently arrived by train—as did other visitors to the area. While passenger service has long been discontinued, the Delaware and Hudson still operates its Adirondack spur over the original route from Saratoga Springs to North Creek.

Visitors to the Adirondack Museum in Blue Mountain Lake may recall the diorama depicting a very special moment in North Creek's past: a weary and somber Theodore Roosevelt on the lantern-lit station platform taking the Presidential oath. To this day, the station looks much the same.

"Barton Mines owns it now," said the young man checking a switch. "They use the back part of the building for storage."

How long will this bit of history be here?

At North River, another man of destiny, Senator Robert Kennedy, visited one spring to participate in the Whitewater Derby on the Upper Hudson. The rapids area rarely freezes, and despite the cold weather, this year is no exception.

20

Today the water churns mean; smoke curls from the chimney of the general store. It's a long time to August when the ladies of the Methodist Church will again display their quilts at the roadside craft fair. A pulp truck passes where a generation before logs were swept by the swift current of spring to the mills in Glens Falls. The last river run was in 1951.

But North River still has its mine—which is more than Witherbee, Lyon Mountain and the other mining towns in the Adirondacks can say. Garnet deposits were discovered here over a century ago. Some of the early crystals were said to be the size of a bushel basket. Mines have been located at Ruby Mountain, Thirteenth Lake and Gore Mountain. Barton Mines Corporation recently proposed development of its land on Gore Mountain into a ski complex, adjoining the state facility on the opposite side of the mountain. Meanwhile, mining operations have returned to Ruby Mountain, and North River continues to produce a large share of the country's commercial-grade garnet.

Now the Hudson bends northward, and Route 28 climbs the big hill. A small car labors to pass. Imagine how difficult it must have been to motor into the woods years ago, before roads were paved, or grades cut? One early motorist reported backing his car up this hill to permit gasoline to flow from tank to carburetor. The incline would not allow forward operation.

New snow has fallen at the higher elevation, just enough to cover the brown on the roadbanks and give the landscape a fresh look. The old log camps along here are still in good repair. Leaden skies promise more winter.

As far as eyes can see, no structure is visible, no sign of man evident—though earlier a snowmobile had autographed the shoulder. With car lights on, snow attacks the windshield, hiding the hills. The start of a winter storm is always exciting. From hilltop, the faint lights of Indian Lake push through darkness and blizzard. They are especially inviting.

The weather report from Schenectady was for an inch or two by morning, and a little more at the higher elevations. At Indian Lake, "a little more" this day translates to better than two feet—enough to have kept the plows working most of the night. Now at daylight, two big town trucks idle at the coffee shop while the crew stops for breakfast. The place was all theirs.

"Blowing in on Crow Hill," said one of the drivers. "By the time I come back, it's filled again."

"Just like you hadn't been there...I know," said another. "It's blowing off the lake, too."

The waitress appeared with heaping plates, more coffee.

"This should fix you up for another four hours," she teased.

"Wanta bet?" That brought a chuckle from the others.

"About now I don't know if I'm too tired to eat, or too hungry to sleep."

"Face it...we're getting too old for this." Talk stopped while the crew attacked their bacon and eggs over lightly with hashbrowns and toast.

A blue pickup with a plow pulled in next to the town trucks.

"Here comes my first customer," said the waitress.

"How about us?" asked the driver.

"You don't count."

Snow swirled around the windows. You could barely see the road.

"You got up before breakfast, I see," greeted the first real customer.

"Like two o'clock," replied one of the crew. "What gets you up so early?"

"I've come to claim my winner. What was yesterday's number?"

The waitress handed him a card listing the winning lottery numbers. He looked at it and shook his head.

"At least I got one number right," he said. Would you punch up this for the big one. I feel lucky."

"It's sixteen million this week, you know," said the waitress.

"OK…I'd better make out two then."

"What are you going to do with all that money anyway?"

"Skip town first of all…just to escape all the friends and relatives I'd suddenly come up with."

"Especially your relatives," chuckled the waitress. "And don't forget who punched the ticket, either. I'll settle for a white Caddie."

"Hey…better run my ticket," said one of the town guys. "Can't let him walk away with all that money."

"I'd settle for just enough to quit this job," said his companion. "But first I've gotta plow out Big Brook."

Now shovels, snowblowers, and pickups were cleaning up where the road crews left off. Once you're past the hard-packed stuff, shoveling comes easy when the snow is dry. Downstate, a storm like this would be a crippler. Here it's just another snow.

Before long, snowmachines were beating a path to Marty's Tavern, and across the back trail to Bear Trap Inn. This is a day for the winter sports to keep fortified.

A pile of snow hides the front window of Spring's Store, reaching almost to the "WORMS" sign beneath the picture of a man snoozing by a potbelly stove. Smoke swirls from the chimney.

A young man shoveled the steps of the hardware.

24

"When you finish there you can start on the sidewalk," said the man carrying a bag of groceries under each arm.

"What sidewalk?" joked the shoveler. "That's the town's snow. They pushed it there. They can carry it away."

"It's good walking in the road. They even sanded it for me."

You can tell when it's mail time. That's when the vehicles descend on the post office. Mostly pick-ups with plows today.

"How did you make it out with that little car?" asked a man.

"Cautiously," chuckled the big woman. "I tell you...if I come back later, it'll be with the snow machine."

The ski tow on Tower Hill wasn't operating, but the kids didn't mind. Somehow they had made it to the top. Now they sailed past balsam heavy with snow, the first skiers of the day. Beyond, a church steeple marked a community hidden from view, trees blended to hills, and a white ribbon of highway wound to the horizon. Currier and Ives could not have found a more fitting winterscape.

In Sabael, the state plow had all but buried the parking area in front of The Lake Store. Along Lake Shore Drive a mound marks the location of a parked car. Nearby, someone leisurely shoveled his way to the road. Perhaps I could take his picture.

"Make sure you get the snow flying," he said. " Don't want people

to think I'm just posing." The soft snow took flight as he briefly attacked the high bank next to the road.

"See that ice shanty down there," He pointed toward the lake. "I want to show this picture to the guy who sits there all day with nothing to do but fish. I want him to see that some people STILL know how to work!"

Snow hides the broken crust of ice at a stream's outlet. Here is where Indian Lake's first resident, Sabael Benedict, had lived. And here is where his woman was said to be buried, at the edge of the ever-flowing Squaw Brook. Even on this day...

The dark, cold water runs free—

past birch, balsam,

and the big boulder.

Restless for a new season.

26

27

OHIO, GRANT, NORTHWOOD, WILMURT, WILMURT CORNERS, GRAY, NOBLEBORO, HOFFMEISTER, HIGGINS BAY, PISECO, OXBOW LAKE, LAKE PLEASANT

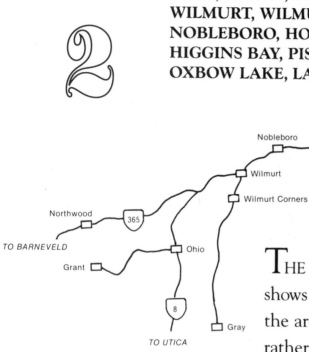

THE entry to the Park northward from Utica on Route 8 shows little promise of the mountains beyond. Officially, the area is considered foothills, but in reality the land is rather flat. The sandy soil here mainly supports scrub birch, pine, brush and a ground cover of moss. Most of the cherry has been logged. These days, the Town of Ohio would hardly be a first choice for farming.

Yet according to one story, the first settlers here had high expectations of the land. Apparently, the speculator who came to call the area Ohio knew full well the marketing value of that name. Of course the unwitting homesteaders who bought his parcels had heard glowing reports of the lush lands in the Buckeye State. One can only imagine their reaction when this bleak foothills acreage first came into view! Undaunted, several of these hardy souls actually stayed on, naming their settlement Ohio City—an expression of defiance, one might suspect.

Ohio City lies just off the highway behind Hotel Ohio. Maybe someone around town can confirm, or deny, this yarn about the first settlers. Perhaps the woman who's peeking at you through the smoke-smudged window, or the owner of the howling dogs down the street? Somehow you sense a stranger's not going to be told the real story about Ohio City's origin even if it were known. OK. Maybe that wasn't a good idea. Maybe you should just mind your own business, and walk down the middle of the road looking straight ahead like you don't see the woman at the window or hear the howling dogs.

Sure enough, that seemed to work. Soon the woman stopped peeking, the dogs stopped barking....and an elderly man appeared at a side door with a bucket of ashes.

"Never was much farming," he told me, spreading the ashes along

the driveway. Dust flew. A hot coal sputtered as it hit the packed snow.

"Can't even grow rocks here."

I hadn't heard that phrase before.

"Just dig into the ground," he explained. "Bet you can't find a rock if you tried."

This time of year it was hard to think of digging into much of anything but snow. Quickly the old man had enough conversation with a stranger to last till spring.

"Better check my traps," he said, revving up the Ski-Doo.

"They say it's going to snow."

Not many cities where you can go trapping, I thought, continuing my walk through Ohio City—past the Ohio Methodist Church and the Olive Branch Garden Club. Stone grave markers peeked through the snow, many tilted by the years. Ohio's early settlers must be buried here.

Surely they knew all about trapping, rabbit hunting— just about everything people still do, except for the machines and TV. Surely they knew the tricks of winter survival, too…like building near the road, and pitching the roof. Snow shoveling was no more fun then than now. Soon the dogs started howling again. I knew it was time to leave.

One senses a lingering frontier quality in this town, even though

Utica is only a half hour away. Ohio is typical of many places in the Adirondacks—a large area inhabited by few people. Law enforcement is provided by the State Police operating from their station in Herkimer, some twenty-five miles to the south. Still, country people sometimes feel the need to do their own protecting. Maybe that's why there are so many dogs around houses.

There's a special day in the spring when people in the area gather to celebrate the coming of the black flies. This ritual, of course, is not quite like the return of the swallows to Capistrano or even the chimney swifts to Northville.

Black flies don't migrate. They just float around in the streams as larvae, waiting for a good warm day to hatch. But sure enough, they do hatch—and that's the cue for people here to start talking up the Black Fly Festival.

Best, though, to let the black flies get a head start before the festival starts. That makes an easier job of picking the Black Fly Queen. The Queen, you see, is chosen not for beauty or talent—though she may excel in both—but for the number of votes cast by the black flies themselves during the outdoor event. The contestant with the highest bite count is crowned Queen. Bet the sovereign state of Ohio couldn't come up with anything more democratic than that.

But on this day more dark than light, the rites of spring are a distant promise. The TV weatherman from Syracuse used to call these dark skies the "great gray funk." He quit the area and is now in Florida, still guessing the weather. But at least he sees the sun this time of year.

Grant is just down Ohio-Pardeeville Road and across the town line into Russia. After a right turn at Pardeeville Corners you're there. Usually there's not much reason to head this way, unless you have relatives in Grant—or you drive the school bus which has just stopped to pick up the children.

Black Creek flows past Grant into Hinckley Reservoir, a fact worthy of note only because Black Creek has been designated a wilderness stream. This means, among other things, that no new construction can take place within a half mile of Black Creek. New construction around Grant appears to be confined to beavers. They need no approval to build along the banks of their stream.

The roads in town are well plowed and sanded, as is the parking area in front of the Grant Hotel. But shortly beyond the hotel, the sanded road gives way to two parallel tracks leading up Stormy Hill Road.

Whenever a strange car heads up Stormy Hill this time of year, one suspects the patrons at the hotel bar place their bets on whether they'll see the car headed back, or the driver walking back. Those parallel tracks were not made by cars or pickups as they might appear, but by snowmobiles—the only sure transportation over Stormy Hill these days. Somewhere along the road, buried in a bank no doubt, is a sign explaining the limits of this seasonal trail.

Grant is best visited in summer. That's when the campers and fishermen drop into the hotel for a beer or two and a good meal.

Route 365 hugs the north shore of Hinckley Reservoir, following the course of an old right-of-way for a proposed railroad extension from Hinckley to Northwood. Northwood was the site of considerable industrial activity in years past. Charcoal and wood-product chemicals were produced here before the reservoir was created by the damming of West Canada Creek. Today there are a few mobile homes and camps along the road, and a boys' camp which retains the Northwood name. A road to the north leads to the settlement of Wheelertown and through the North Wilmurt region to Atwell on North Lake.

The few houses of Wilmurt along Route 8 and Wilmurt Corners are separated by a beautifully wild strip of West Canada Creek on the Gray-Wilmurt Road. As the road bumps its way toward Gray, it passes a sawmill where some building logs are for sale.

Log construction is popular in the area. The logs, usually red pine, are prepared by squaring two sides to a uniform thickness of six inches. The material removed during squaring is sawed into 2 x 4s and 2 x 6s for use in framing. After the remaining bark is peeled, the logs are stacked and allowed to air dry.

The building technique is equally simple. Strips of fiberglass insulation are placed between layers of logs, which are secured every three or four feet with 12-inch spikes. Doors and windows are framed with 2 x 8s or 2 x 10s, and large nails driven into the ends of abutting logs. At the corners, log ends are shaped with a chain saw to match the contour of adjacent logs, and insulation packed between the two. Corner logs normally are staggered in the traditional manner.

In Gray, all roads lead to The Gray Store. It's the focal point of the area, a place to pick up a few items between trips to Utica, and maybe say hello to a neighbor. The Gray Store is famous for cheese. The sharp cheddar has a real nip and the extra sharp, well….it bites. Should be sold with a warning, some say.

"How do you get cheese to taste like this?" I asked. I felt I was asking Betty Crocker to reveal her innermost secret.

"Just keep it on the shelf," I was told. "Then…when you think it's ready to sell, keep it on the shelf a while longer."

Two teenage girls were discussing cars and boyfriends. They moved from one subject to the other with ease.

"He's putting in a 405," said the girl in the red jacket. "You still have that four barrel? Billy wants it."

The second girl nodded. "But it needs a good cleaning. Hey...we're going down to Herkimer tonight with Ron. Wanta come?"

Outside, a three-wheeler rounded the corner and headed out of the Park toward Norway. A few moments later, a snowmobile crossed over the bare strip of road in front of the fire hall, then back onto the bank in the direction of Buff Hill. Right now there's more traffic from sporting machines than cars around Gray. But then, Gray's a sporting place, especially on the opening day of deer season. That's when the women in town put on their turkey dinner with all the fixings, right down to the homebaked pies. Some say that about half the people who come up for hunting that day really come to get the meal over at the fire barn. I don't doubt it.

Route 8 crosses West Canada Creek at Nobleboro, a settlement dating from 1787, the year Arthur Noble was assigned two parcels by the State Legislature. After constructing a road and a sawmill his effort at settlement was abandoned. Today the area is marked by a bridge across the creek and a few houses. A large flag is stretched between two trees at one camp, providing the only touch of color this bleak day.

A pickup passed at the Hamilton County line, kicking sand and slush in its wake. Quickly it disappeared around the bend, hell-bent toward Speculator. That driver must be a stranger. Anyone who knows the road would have waited for the flat, level stretch just ahead.

Route 8 is more than a through road. It's Main Street for the Town of Morehouse, passing the few dwellings and brush- covered fields which once were farms. Today, Morehouse has but a handful of people—mostly surrounding the settlement of Hoffmeister where the post office is located, and a vacated store weathers another winter.

This was not exactly the vision Andrew Morehouse had for his town. A man with imagination and a tremendous capacity for work, Morehouse dreamed of a prosperous community surrounded by farms—linked by rail with the lush markets to the south. His untiring efforts to bring settlers to the area met with early success. By the 1850s the town could claim seven sawmills, a gristmill, two retail stores, two inns, two churches—and a population of 250. But when Andrew Morehouse's efforts to secure a rail route through the town failed, his enthusiasm for the area faltered and the town went into hibernation.

Half way through the 20th century, electricity came to Morehouse, the last town in the Empire State to receive power from a utility. The event, which brought both joy and tears to the town's few remaining residents, was duly reported by the big city papers. Gone at last were the old storage-battery radios dating from the 20's, the smoking oil lamps, the noisy generator puffing power from the woodshed. Refrigerators quickly replaced ice boxes, and TV antennas sprouted from rooftops. Overnight, the whole world of electrified convenience and entertainment came to Morehouse.

Today, few who pass this way would give passing notice to the power lines along this flat stretch of Route 8. But the old-timers in town will never forget that Holiday Season in 1953 when the lights came on—an event beyond Andrew Morehouse's finest dream.

The pickup which had passed in a cloud of slush now was parked in front of Bear Path Inn, along with another car and two snowmobiles. Guess the driver knew where he was going, after all.

The cottages and camps of Higgins Bay wait patiently for spring and the return of the trout fishermen. Piseco has attracted anglers forever, it seems. As early as 1830, members of the Piseco Lake Trout Club were making the arduous journey to their wilderness retreat. Once the club reported a catch of over 900 pounds in nine days on the lake. That's serious fishing.

But then, people here have always taken their trout fishing seriously. One of the old-timers, Floyd Lobb, even designed his own trolling spoon which came into wide use. It is said Lobb's dying request was to fish

while being rowed across the lake. Using his favorite spoon, he managed to hook two lake trout. A few days later he was buried at Higgins Bay cemetery together with a collection of his lures.

While the mountain lakes now support fewer fish, Piseco still yields its share of large trout. The HAMILTON COUNTY NEWS recently reported a Mayfield man hauling in a 22-pounder on his first trip of the season to Piseco.

On this winter day, however, the lake belongs to a snowmobile purring toward the hills on the other side where the state campground and small camps share the narrow strip between road and shore.

Andrew Morehouse's Adirondack vision extended to Piseco. He foresaw a planned community on the northern edge of the lake whose neatly-aligned streets would be named for presidents and men of high position. Because a community this exceptional would be selected as the county seat and site of the courthouse, Morehouse's plan for Piseco included a Court Street. Nothing, it appeared was left to chance—except the plan's implementation. Today, there is little evidence any of Morehouse's neatly-structured dream came to pass. The town has a Haskell Road, Dump Road, and Wild Road, but no streets named for presidents. And since the county courthouse came to be located in Lake Pleasant, Piseco had no need for a Court Street, either.

But Piseco does have an airport, the only one in Hamilton County. At the moment, its 3000-foot runway is somewhere under the snow-covered field next to the post office. If a plane lands today, it had better be equipped with skis. Piseco's attractive elementary school is located on Route 8. The community also has a museum. Like much of Piseco, it is closed this time of year. Smoke curls from the chimneys of but a few houses this February day.

Oxbow Lake has been designated a hamlet, according to the road marker on Route 8, and a neatly hand-lettered sign in the window of the Oxbow Diner. The men at the table were talking about road fixing, and town business.

"I wanted to get this done last year," said the first man. "Now it's gonna cost us ten or fifteen percent more."

"That sounds high," said the second man. "Will you have to tear it all up?"

The first man nodded. "Either that...or we'll have to keep doing it every year."

Leaving, I spotted a notice for the Artic Sled Dog Races on the lake. That sounded more interesting than repairing bumps on a back road.

The parking area in front of Oxbow Inn was primed for the

races—Oxbow Lake's biggest event of the season if not the year. A team of samoyeds in harness huddled around a pickup. Nearby, three Siberian huskies peeked from the portholes of their house on wheels, a sled still attached to its roof. From the lake came the happy yelps and howls of a team already running. The samoyeds and huskies quickly joined the chorus. In the woods beyond, the coyotes no doubt wondered what the commotion was all about.

By February, snow piles high in front of the county buildings at Lake Pleasant. The trip down from Inlet or Long Lake takes longer than ever this time of year.

Hamilton County is small only in population, its 5000 residents nearly equally divided between its northern and southern stretches, with a vast wilderness and forest area separating the two. The present Route 30 from Speculator to Indian Lake is the single connecting link between these two areas of the county. It was not until 1955 that the road was paved, and Hamilton County finally joined by a serviceable year-round north-south highway.

On this day, foot traffic at the county seat is mostly up the steps of the County Clerk's Office to the Motor Vehicle Bureau. The courthouse and jail appear settled in for a long winter's nap, or until the peace is disturbed and justice again dispensed.

CORINTH, LAKE LUZERNE, FOURTH LAKE, LAKE VANARE, BEARTOWN, HADLEY, CONKLINGVILLE

By mid-February, road dirt and sand have turned the banks along Route 32 into something other than a picture of beauty. New snow might improve the sight, but only briefly. The best hope lies a few weeks ahead when the sun grows higher, and the rains of early spring wash it all away.

Meanwhile, the season is better viewed from a distance. Hills and fields remain clean, bright. A farmhouse

41

along the way retains late-winter's charm, too—its roof heavy with snow and icicles stretching ever longer. A pretty sight, providing the roof is not yours to shovel, nor icicles yours to remove.

This day is chilly despite the sun. The houses of Corinth huddle along the Hudson's shoreline, seeking cover from the wind. As a siren and horn jointly announce the noon hour, a town truck stopped near the bridge entrance, and lunch pails appeared. Down the street, a passing pickup honked "Hello" to the three men shivering in front of Mosher's Hardware.

"Don't you know enough to get outa the cold?" shouted the driver.

"We're trying to figure out if these snowblowers are going on sale," replied one.

"Don't you know spring's coming?"

The flagpole in front of Corinth's Village Hall displayed more than the Stars and Stripes. Colorfully decorated with symbols and words, the hand-crafted pole admonishes villagers to ETERNAL VIGILANCE, LIBERTY, UNION, EQUAL JUSTICE, and DUTY.

Main Street is alive with activity. At the top of the hill, a mother hurried from the Headstart School, child in hand. Kids tossed snowballs at the procession of cars slowly moving through the business district. Above the street, power and phone lines laced the landscape. The outlying hills appeared caught in this web.

An empty pulp truck headed north, spraying sand, slush—and strains of "Rocky Mountain High" from the local station. Too bad mountain music has to be imported. But then, late winter offers little inspiration for Adirondack songs. It's still survival time in these hills. So John Denver had the airwaves to himself as we bounced northward. Ahead, the town plow ran interference...sparking bare pavement as we passed Lake Luzerne's sign, and Armstrong's Garage where a poster for Big Hat Country awaits summer's guests. Finally the plow stopped at the Diner. Any place the town crew eats must be OK.

The International Paper and Niagara Mohawk crews eat here, too. The place is packed, except for the spot at the counter just vacated by the man with a large cross hanging from a chain.

"He's moving away you know," said the waitress to a hard-hatted customer. "That leaves three churches without a minister, counting the one in Stony Creek."

"Seems like the good ones are gone before you know it," replied the customer. "Hey...what's your special tonight?"

Lake Luzerne is an attractive community—and one of the Adirondacks' oldest. The Jessup Brothers built their first mill here in 1770. The village wears its years well, as a quick walk along a tree-lined

street confirms. The chimney at the old tannery still stands, and across the street a flag flies from the porch of the Francis Garnar Kinnear Museum of Local History.

The two men making repairs on the Town Hall pause in mock interest at the sight of a stranger with a camera.

"Hold it," said one, raising a make-believe camera to his eye.

"Like this?" asked the other, raising a roll of roofing felt above his head. Both laughed at their antics.

A string of buses line up at the elementary school north of the village. Adirondack school districts draw their students from a large area. Hadley-Luzerne is no exception. Nearly all the children attending this school take the bus.

Route 9N may have lost its through traffic to the Northway. Still, it thrives on local trade. The parking lot of the Potash Inn at Fourth Lake is filled with snow machines. Several others "w-h-i-r-r-r" over the ice of Lake Vanare. This time of year the resorts along Hidden Valley Road make their living from snowmobilers.

Never have I heard anyone say they came from Beartown, or were headed there. Yet Beartown was on the map, just off the road between Lake Luzerne and West Glens Falls. Trouble was, I couldn't find a roadsign pointing the way. Guess it's one of those places where only a stranger would expect to see a sign.

On a hunch, I turned onto a side road barely wide enough for a car to pass. A road like this could lead to a place called Beartown, I reasoned. Besides, it was plowed and sanded—even if utility lines were missing.

Before long the winding road tackled a steep hill. With a wary eye, I peeked into a deep ravine and hugged the opposite bank as the car struggled upward. Will Beartown ever come? How many houses will there be? Could it possibly have a store or church? Finally the grade leveled and I arrived at a turnaround. Still no buildings. Nothing but a logging road ahead.

"What are you doing up this way?"

Surprised, I turned to the direction of the voice. At the edge of the logging road stood a ranger.

"There's a few camps further down," he said, "but you won't get there unless you have your own plow. One guy plows his way in."

"Doesn't look like he's been up this year," I said. So how come the road up is plowed?"

"International Paper is doing some logging. Hey…here comes another car."

"Guess Beartown's getting a real traffic jam. Three vehicles."

"And there's more than us here," said the excited driver, sliding as

45

he hit the brakes. "Just spotted a wolf down the road."

That brought a "H-m-m-m" from the ranger who knew there were no wolves in these woods.

"Maybe a coyote," he answered. "Plenty of those around."

That was reassuring. At least Beartown has some residents up and about this time of year, even if they're not people—or bears.

Hadley lies in the shadow of Lake Luzerne—just across the bridge. One place blends to the other. Hadley remains unannounced until you reach the top of the hill. And by the time you read that Hadley was established in 1801, you're hardly there anymore. Even so, you get the idea this place remains independent of its neighbor across the Hudson. Hadley has a post office of its own, an Agway store, and town hall where the afternoon sun has loosened snow from the metal roof. With a loud "s-s-w-i-s-h," a sheet of white slid to the ground, briefly disrupting the quiet. People here don't question the value of a pitched metal roof. Nor the need to stay clear of overhangs when snow starts to melt.

A sign pointed the way to Conklingville along the Sacandaga on Route 4, past a logging area, and up a hill to a turn-off overlooking the Great Sacandaga Lake. Directly below, the Conklingville dam stretches 1100 feet across the head of the reservoir.

But today all eyes at the turnoff are directed to the trees across the river where bald eagles have been wintering.

"These birds are opportunists," said the man with both binoculars and camera strapped around his neck. "They'd just as soon take a fish that's gone through the turbine as a live one."

"Guess this is a good spot for them," I said.

"Open water, food, privacy...they've got it all," said the expert.

Another car stopped. The place was quickly filling. Guess that story in the Albany paper about the eagles had brought the bird-watchers out.

"What's the man looking at?" asked a child.

"He's looking for a big bird," answered the father.

"I can't see Big Bird," said the child, expecting his friend from Sesame Street.

This was not the best of days for eagle watching. But spirits still soared, if not the birds...especially so with the well-equipped family at the station wagon. They did their eagle-searching as a team: mother and son scanning pre-defined areas with binoculars, and father at the ready with his telephoto camera on a window tripod.

"I've got one!" exclaimed the son.

"Where? Where?" asked father, peering through the viewfinder of his monster camera.

"I can't see it," said mother. "Is it that bump?"

Down on the reservoir side of the dam, an ice fisherman cracked another beer, oblivious of the drama above. A sign on the building nearby said DAY COUNTRY STORE.

"Isn't this Conklingville?" I asked.

"Mostly, Conklingville's right here," replied the fisherman, stomping his foot on the ice. "After the place got flooded, they started to call it Day, because the Town of Day was about all that was left."

"How about the church?"

"You're right. That's the Community Church of Conklingville."

I left Conklingville satisfied it was still more than a dam.

"Mostly Conklingville's right here," replied the fisherman.

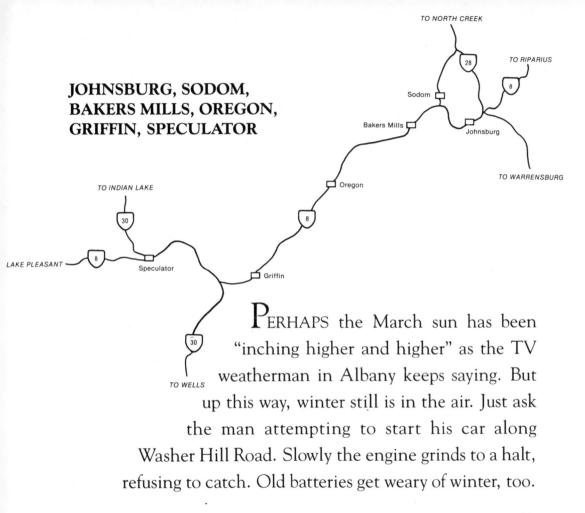

JOHNSBURG, SODOM, BAKERS MILLS, OREGON, GRIFFIN, SPECULATOR

Perhaps the March sun has been "inching higher and higher" as the TV weatherman in Albany keeps saying. But up this way, winter still is in the air. Just ask the man attempting to start his car along Washer Hill Road. Slowly the engine grinds to a halt, refusing to catch. Old batteries get weary of winter, too.

49

Cold weather is nothing new to Johnsburg. The place has been around long enough to have seen it all. At one time Johnsburg was even mentioned as a possible site for the State Capitol. That's the story some tell. It must been a long winter when that idea was hatched.

Today Johnsburg's homes and stores share a bit of Route 8. Mill Creek Bait and Tackle is here, along with the Johnsburg Public Market, and a liquor store. Nearby, a contractor's equipment peeks from the snow, awaiting spring. The United Methodist Church dates from 1838. Many of Johnsburg's early residents are buried in the adjoining cemetery. Nearby is a stately old house—another reminder of the town's past.

No sign shows the way to Sodom, but directions are simple: just drive along Peaceful Valley Road until you see a group of mailboxes. The mailman makes one stop in Sodom.

Other than a steeple and worn stone steps, Sodom's church shows little evidence of its heritage. These days, curtains hang from plain glass windows. Perhaps those who settled here from Putnam County would recognize their house of worship.

The woodpiles of Bakers Mills are shrinking fast. When will winter end? The man shoveling the layers of January and February from a flat roof would like to know. So would the old-timer spreading ashes along the road at the Pentecostal Holiness-P.H.A. Church.

"Can't remember when I've used this much wood," he said.

I heard Bakers Mills was called Dogtown. But no dogs were around.

"Too cold for the dogs?" I asked.

"Just go over to Zero Kennels. Bet you'll find a hundred sled dogs there."

No doubt the bear population is high, too—especially along the Siamese Pond Wilderness Area which extends to Route 8. From roadside you can see the wilderness markers. Carving pasture from forest was never easy. Only a few farms remain.

Road maps still mark the location of Oregon. You'd expect to find a community—or something. True, the entrance to the former Hudnut estate is here—hidden today by snow. But Fox Lair was burned by the state some years ago, and the land returned to wilderness. Only garden walls and staircases remain, I am told. Here, too, was the Oregon tannery, destroyed by fire in 1892. Some names outlive their places. Oregon is one.

Griffin is another. Once Griffin was a thriving community of some 300 people, with stores, two hotels, a bar, a telegraph office, a post office, and a school. A large tannery was here. But with the advent of chemical tanning, the fate of Griffin was sealed.

Today, the iron bridge crossing the East Branch of the Sacandaga

marks Griffin's location. New growth covers much of the former community. In most places civilization overtakes wilderness. At Griffin it's the other way around.

The highway north follows a ridge of white birch along Sacandaga's Middle Branch, bypassing the old road leading to Gilmantown. A pickup sped by, spraying melting road mix. Moments later it turned off at Camp-of-the-Woods.

The Speculator area has always attracted visitors. Soon after the first settlers arrived, sportsmen came to Lake Pleasant, lured by reports of huge trout and an abundance of wildfowl, deer and other game. Newton Corners, as the settlement which developed at the foot of the lake came to be called, showed great promise. By the end of the 19th century, a new breed of vacationer flocked to the area from the cities to the south. In an attempt to find a name better suited to this market, Newton Corners became Speculator.

Still, the corner is Speculator's hub of commerce. You'll find places to shop, eat, sleep, bank, or do the laundry—all within a few feet. The Speculator Department Store, a long-time shopping favorite for tourists, is here. So is Zeiser's Inn. Across the street is Charles Johns Store, an independent supermarket with a general store flavor.

Speculator was among the first communities in the state to promote winter sports. Bobsled runs, ice skating, skiing, and hockey were all here. Today, the Oak Mountain Ski Center continues the tradition.

A busload of children just arrived from Northville. Quickly kids swarmed to the lift. Nearby, an excited father aims a camcorder toward his daughter. You know it's her first run ever.

"OK....let's do it!" called dad from the foot of the bunny slope. "Hang in now!

Down the gentle slope came his little girl, arms outstretched and giggling as she hit a bump.

"WOOPS..." exclaimed father, recording for posterity a surprised child in a snowbank with skis crossed and cap hiding an eye.

Now...as fresh winds bring new snow, another surprise unfolds at the Speculator Department Store.

"Just wait here," said the wife to her husband. "I'll only be a minute."

The husband nodded as she left the van, knowing there was no such thing as a minute in a store with a SALE. Soon he settled back with the Glens Falls paper: the Knicks had lost...the Middle East was in turmoil...and so was Congress. Everything's about the same, he thought, glancing through the mirror in the direction of the store. No wife. So back to the news he went. A convenience store in Saratoga had been

robbed of thirty-five bucks…Granville received three bids for a new town truck…and a study commision for…"Ho-hum." With a yawn, he set the paper aside and shut his eyes.

A snowmobile woke him as it sputtered down the driveway, but he could only hear it. Snow covered the windows of the van. Deciding it was time to start home, the husband entered the store in search of his salemate.

The place was empty, not counting the clerk who silently stared out at the swirling snow. Back he walked…past sporting goods and men's wear. No wife. Nothing…except a dim light escaping from the dressing room on the other side.

"Is that you in there?" he called.

"Come here," answered his wife from the behind the door. "I want to show you something."

As the husband approached, with cheeks still flushed from his brief encounter with the mounting blizzard, his wife flung open the dressing room door…attired in high socks, winter boots—and a bathing suit!

The surprised husband, who was not thinking bathing beauties on this day, let forth a "WOW!" which shook the rafters of Speculator's Department Store. Even the clerk spun around.

"It's half price," said the unflappable wife. "My goodness…I think you're blushing!" A smile came over her face. When was the last time she had seen him blush?

Recovering, the husband merely nodded. Why even suggest the redness of cheeks was more blizzard than blush? And yes…why spoil his vision of Speculator's late-winter bathing beauty? Tomorrow at the coffee shop he'll remember…and next month during mud season. Surely that image will remain even when black flies hatch in May.

Shuffling back to the van, he could swear the drifting snow was a beach.

"Eat your heart out, Fort Lauderdale,"

he murmured…

brushing fluffy white stuff

from the windows.

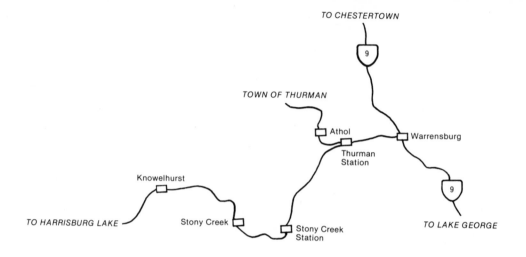

WARRENSBURG
THURMAN STATION
ATHOL
THURMAN
STONY CREEK STATION
STONY CREEK
KNOWELHURST

WARRENSBURG is large or small, depending on the road you take to town. If you're driving up the Northway from Albany, it's just another little place along the road, a turn-off for gas or a Big Mac. Then quickly you're back on the highway—Exit 23 skiddoo!

But enter Warrensburg from one of the roads winding down from the hills. Now the place looms big. Shops and stores of every description, large beautifully restored houses—even a park with bandstand named for its native son and aviation pioneer, Floyd Bennett. Here's a place that's got about everything you can get in Glens Falls without going the extra miles. People in this niche of the woods hold a loyalty to Warrensburg. It's their kind of town.

This late-winter day, a pulp truck rolls down Main Street splashing road slush onto the sidewalk. An elderly man headed for Richards Library quickly tucked a book under his coat. Down the street, a mother and daughter leave the Riverside Gallery, glancing briefly at the store's display of toy sheep. Nearby, the Schroon River flows fast and cold beneath the bridge where the ducks hide between feedings. Some of the earliest mills in the Adirondacks were along the Schroon. The old gristmill now is a restaurant, and a rambling factory building a wholesale outlet. Others have long since disappeared.

But Warrensburg remembers its past. Back in the 1970s, Eva Cockroft, Jim Cockroft and Dick Doux erected scaffolding alongside the Odd-Fellows building on Main Street to paint a mural depicting the early years of the community. They titled it: WARRENSBURGH A TOWN IN HARMONY WITH ITS PAST. These days vacationers walk the streets instead of loggers, and antique shops have replaced the mills. The mural portrays a Yankee peddler traveling a plank road. Now tractor

57

trailers speed along the Northway with their wares. Just about everything has changed.

Each fall Warrensburg goes retail in a big way. That's when the community hosts a merchandising extravaganza billed as the World's Largest Garage Sale. Flea market operators, merchants, antiquers, junktiquers—and anyone else with something to sell—set up their booths. The whole town prays for good weather that weekend.

"Gives you a chance to buy just about anything you don't need," said the glum-faced man at the diner.

"Hey Smiley," called the waitress from the Silex machine. "You look like another cup of coffee."

"Sure hope I don't look like this stuff," replied the man with an ever-so-slight smile.

"Careful now, Smiley. Don't want your face to crack." Both laughed.

One suspects such patter is routine at the diner— especially this time of year when you think spring but still see winter. Soon now the people in town will be waiting for the fruit stand to set out the flats of marigolds and petunias. That's when spring officially arrives in Warrensburg. Meanwhile, counter punching at the diner helps to pass the time—even if it doesn't melt the snow or dry the mud.

58

Route 418 takes the easy way out of Warrensburg, tracking the Schroon River to its union with the Hudson at Thurman Station. Along the way, horses huddle in their small roadside corral at Sit 'n Bull Ranch, one of many dude ranches in the area. This is a relaxed time of year at the ranch, before the cowboys from downstate return.

The Adirondack spur of the Delaware and Hudon Railroad hugs the Hudson on its trek from Corinth to North Creek. At Thurman Station, the tracks thread past a few homes, an operating farm or two, and the open fields stretching to the hills. Ahead the road turns lonely, and the old Esso map didn't help.

"Is Athol this way?" I asked a snow shoveler.

"You want Athol?" An especially long "A" corrected my error. Then a pause to let a stranger's mistake sink in. "Back down the road and to the right."

The road to Athol was clear, rolling past open fields and wooded areas. At a roadside farm, a horse peeked curiously from behind a snowbank. Few cars pass this way. Soon I came upon a settlement unannounced by sign. This must be Athol. But up the street I spotted a sign posted at an attractive Victorian house: THURMAN COMMUNITY CENTER. If this is Thurman, what's happened to Athol? No one was around to solve the mystery. So I continued driving.

Now the road twisted past homes, camps, and through a stand of young hardwood where a partridge took flight—barely clearing the car. Then more scattered houses with BEWARE OF DOG signs, but no dogs. Or people.

Backtracking, I stopped at a cement block building where a truck, car, payloader, and two snowmobiles were parked. A small sign above the entrance said this was BAKER'S GARAGE ATHOL N.Y. I could hear the thud of hammer on metal within. OK...now's my chance to solve this riddle!

"I'm looking for Thurman." I said, attempting to sound like I wasn't totally lost. The two figures bent over an engine in the corner smiled at each other.

"You're here...smack in the middle of it," said one.

"Your sign says Athol." That was my best long "A."

"That's right. Athol is in the middle of Thurman," said the other. I sensed they were having fun with me. How could anyone be here and not know it?

"You mean this is the Town of Thurman?"

"Sure is. Even included Warrensburg in the old days."

The other guy looked out the window. "Here comes the supervisor," he said. "Bet he can help you."

"Tell him how to get to Thurman," said the first guy, nudging the supervisor.

"Who in Thurman you want to see?"

Bet he does know everyone around here, I thought. "No one really," I finally admitted. "Just wanted to see where Thurman was."

"Well...take any road. We go all the way up to Johnsburg, and down to Stony Creek."

Leaving Baker's Garage in Athol, Town of Thurman, I knew I needed a better map before venturing down another back road.

A few weeks later I was on my way again, with a detailed map of the Adirondacks in hand. Even if I hadn't been on the road to Stony Creek before, I felt comfortable with every dip and turn. They were all on the map—except for the bumps.

These days the snows of midwinter are crusted and packed. Gone is the clean beauty of winter's cover. Small branches dropped by earlier winds peek through the snow; rocks and bare patches appear. Stony Creek is open, running wild.

At Stony Creek Station, a roadside building advertises antiques and cabinetry. Nearby, two children slide down a brown snowbank on a day there isn't much else to do. The water roared beneath the bridge, carrying limbs, branches and the ice of yesterday's breakup.

Further upstream at the village, an old man paused on the porch of the general store to survey the scene. All was quiet at the Stony Creek Inn where a sign in front promises REAL FOOD and a MEXICAN MENU SUNDAYS. No doubt the place will be jumping on Monday. That's St. Patrick's Day.

Melting snow has puddled the road in front of the store with the AMMO sign. Nearby the Stars and Stripes waves in the breeze. Plows have already been taken off three of the town trucks—as sure a sign of the changing season as the breakup of the creek. Down the street, two young men huddled beneath the hood of a car, undisturbed by the shrill sound of the noon whistle. Now the old man at the store decided it was time to head for the restaurant. But not to the eating side.

Laughter and spirited conversation floated from the drinking side. A gravelly voice rose above the noise, recounting a story already well known. But that didn't spoil the punch line:

"So he says 'Where are you?' 'HERE,' she says... 'UNDER the porch you damned fool!'" The drinking side exploded with howls.

Soon a big lady appeared with an Electrolux. Bright green polyester slacks announced she was ready for St. Patrick's Day.

"You're not going to run that thing in here, are you?" asked the man at the pool table. "If I want to hear that noise I'd go home."

Again howls. Laughs came easily today. So the pool player repeated his joke. The Electrolux lady laughed, too, as she moved the wand back and forth over the small entrance rug. The vacuum sounded right at home with the gravelly voice, and the country music from the jukebox.

Stony Creek has its more reserved side, I am sure. Still, it seems to be a place where even a quiet March Saturday is cause for celebration. Wonder what St. Patrick's Day will bring? Or Stony Creek Days next summer?

The road to Knowelhurst and Harrisburg Lake passes the Gun Club, crossing the creek and skirting a steep hill. Along the way, cows huddled near a barn where a man looked over his shoulder to see if friend or stranger was passing. He waved. Beyond a hill rutted with the remains of winter is the Knowelhurst Baptist Church. In the cemetery nearby, a flag marked the gravesite of Jonathan Knowlton.

A plowed driveway leads across the field to a single farmhouse and barn set at the edge of the woods. There may be other year-round residents, but not along Darling Road which is untouched by plow after a few hundred feet. Today...

Knowelhurst relaxes in the
quiet beauty of winter's end.

WELLS
HOPE
HOPE FALLS
NORTHVILLE

By March, just about everyone in the Adirondacks is convinced mountain trails were never meant to be paved. In a few weeks, when ground finally thaws and macadam settles, motoring again will be smoother. For now, however, one place in the woods is usually a hop, skip, and a bump from the next.

Surprisingly, winter has been kind to Route 30 south

of Speculator. There's hardly a jolt to be felt in this stretch through Griffin Gorge, past the "Welcome to Wells" sign, and across the bridge. Today, the Sacandaga runs open to Lake Algonquin.

About half way between bridge and dam is Community Hall. Wells' 180th birthday is being celebrated, the sign in front says. Wells is the oldest town in Hamilton County. Next summer, under the red-covered pavilion in the field nearby, Old Home Days will again honor the community's agricultural and lumbering past. The community is proud of its heritage. Too bad their covered bridge is gone. But the old schoolhouse still sits in the middle of town, its bell intact. These days kids are bussed to a modern school on the edge of the village. The new bell system is electrical, no doubt. That's progress.

Two snowmobilers race across open fields behind a restaurant—in no hurry for winter to end. But the young man feeding the woodstove in the corner will welcome warmer days.

"You're always carrying in wood," said the man at the counter.

"Or carrying out ashes. Hey…wasn't it your truck that hit a deer?"

"Yep…about this much was left." The customer pointed to his half-consumed hamburger.

The young man stared at the customer's plate. "Tell me…is that hamburger the deer or your truck?"

A few miles south on Route 30 is the Sacandaga campground, one of the first in the area. Today, picnic tables tilt at parade rest; a lone telephone booth stands guard over the snow-covered campsite.

The houses of Hope stretch along the east side of the road from the Alpine Inn to Old Northville Road. The abandoned farms across the river hold memories of a bygone era along Hope Valley—of planting, mowing, milking and other labors of the land. People now drive to places like Gloversville, Amsterdam, or Schenectady for work. Much has changed around here...but not everything.

Steam still rises from a sugar shed along the road. "MAPLE SYRUP $4/QUART" reads a dusty sign in the nearby garage.

"Looking for syrup?" came a voice from the loft.

"I see you're boiling today," I replied. "Smells good."

A young man climbed down from the loft. "Should be ready Saturday," he said. "I'll get four dollars again this year."

"Fair enough."

"Some people get seven or eight dollars. But I get my wood free. Helps keep the price down."

The wood, mostly pine, was stacked on either side of the shed. Concrete blocks lined the fire pit, supporting two metal sap trays. The sweet aroma of sap steam gently punched through the shed. The young man scooped boiling liquid from the first tray, adding to that in the second tray.

"I'm boiling it down in two stages," he told me. "This time of year it takes about 45 gallons of sap to make a gallon of syrup. Later on the sap's not as sweet. Might take 55 gallons then."

"That's a lot of hauling."

"Not bad with the snow machine. Besides, I'm only tapping 80 trees this year."

He paused to dip raw sap from a galvanized pail into the first tray.

"That's state land back there," he said, pointing with the scoop. "Thousands of maples, but we can't touch them. They used to issue permits, but no more."

He added more wood to the fire. The dry pine snapped and sparked.

"If I had a larger operation I'd get an evaporator. There's a guy down in Edinburg who makes a thousand gallons a season."

"He's got help, of course."

"And overhead. But I like it this way. Learned how from my father. Now we have a little guy. Guess I'll be teaching him one of these days."

Along the Old Northville Road, a sign pointed the way to Hope Falls, and the two dogs lunking in the middle of Creek Road. They were

in no hurry to move. At the clearing beyond the hill a boy stood at a mailbox.

"Is this the road to Hope Falls?" I asked.

"Yep...this was it. The tannery was down the road a half mile."

I wondered why he spoke in past tense. "What else is here?" I inquired.

"Well...that was the schoolhouse right there," he said, pointing to the building across the road. "And on top of the hill was the old cemetery."

Someone had added a cement block chimney to the front of the school, and had started to stain the sides brown. Curtains hung from the windows. Who would guess this metal-roofed building had once been a place of learning?

Time might alter schools, but not cemeteries—even if the years do erase the shallow inscriptions from some of the markers. Many of Hope Falls' early settlers were put to rest on this knoll behind the school. Here and there a grave is marked with a field stone. Near the stone wall at one side now tangled with vines is said to be the unmarked grave of Edward Earl, the only person to be hung in Hamilton County. Here, too, are the remains of Mary Earl, the wife he murdered with a tannery knife on a winter's night in 1881. Today, there is no evidence of either grave. What other secrets might be hidden here, I wondered? Finally, a crow broke the silence.

Back on Old Northville Road, a hayrack rests in the fertile valley between hill and river. Much of the farmland to the south had been flooded when the reservoir was created. This area was spared.

Approaching Northville, the terrain changes from mountains to hills, from woods to fields. There's a difference within the community, too. The businessmen lunching at the Alhambra wear ties and jackets, and talk about sales calls in Albany. Further north, you don't see many people dressed for the city, talking business.

A day in late winter doesn't come any better than this one to Northville. Just ask the old man relaxing at the doorway on the sunny side of the street, or the mother pushing a stroller past the sidewalk display of shovels and ice choppers at Allen and Palmer. They can tell you all about gray skies and wet snow—the more usual fare this time of year. Little wonder there's a quickness to mother's step as she eyes the Easter candies at J. J. Newberry and the hand-lettered signs announcing 20% off on yarns and fabrics at Dodge's Department Store. Spring is in the air. Even the dormant flies in the window at Lewek's Drugstore are coming to life. Their movement delights the child in the stroller who points with glee as they crawl across the display of old-time remedies in the window.

Gradually, the snowbanks of Northville are shrinking. Here and there on a south-facing slope, grass peeks through the crusted cover of winter. Still, it's a long time to May when the chimney swifts return. People here say their arrival is a big event—bringing out the high school band and half the county. One year a reporter was here from the NEW YORK TIMES, and NBC sent a camera crew to tape the birds' return from South America.

Right on schedule, the chimney swifts swooped in at dusk, circled for the cameras while they formed a funnel, then dove into the 50-foot stack at the old glove factory. When spring finally comes to Northville, it arrives in style.

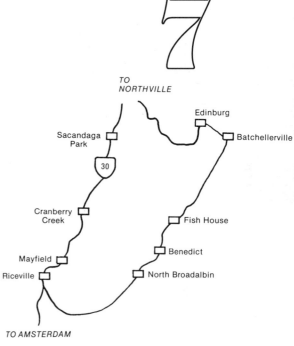

TO
NORTHVILLE

Edinburg

Sacandaga
Park

Batchellerville

30

Cranberry
Creek

Fish House

Benedict

Mayfield

Riceville

North Broadalbin

TO AMSTERDAM

EDINBURG, BATCHELLERVILLE, FISH HOUSE, BENEDICT, NORTH BROADALBIN, RICEVILLE, MAYFIELD, CRANBERRY CREEK, SACANDAGA PARK

THE Sacandaga Region is one area of the Adirondacks not dominated by mountains or forest. Here the reservoir, or Great Sacandaga Lake as it was named, is king. It rules the area geographically, economically—at times politically. Geologists say a lake existed here centuries ago but was gradually transformed into the giant marshland known as the Vly. When the gates for the Conklingville Dam were closed

71

in 1930 and the wetlands flooded, man reversed Nature's course. The Sacandaga became a born-again lake.

The road to Edinburg from Northville rises to higher ground and the settlements of Carpenter Corners and Fairchild Corners. Corners are always named it seems, even if known only to a few neighbors.

Roads are usually named, too—though rarely do they have numbers. "Oh...he lives out Olaf Johnson Road," someone might say. "It's the house with a pile of firewood." So you travel a back road from one end to the other, spotting woodpiles cut or uncut, split or unsplit, in practically every yard. Sometimes it's easier to write a person you seek and address the envelope "Local." One way or another, the mailman will find the right woodpile for you.

You don't need the mailman to find Plateau Sky Ranch Airport. Just follow the sign down the side road until you come to a single-engine plane tethered at the edge of the runway. Nor do you need help finding the old sawmill in Edinburg. Just look for snow brown with sawdust, and a building that's been around forever.

"Don't know exactly how old it is," said the younger of two men looking over a pile of logs. "Been here as long as I know."

"Maybe longer," said the other, watching with amusement as I kicked at a pile of sawdust and discovered mostly ice.

"Don't you remember how they used to keep ice in sawdust?" he joked. "That hunk will be around till summer."

Edinburg was first called Beecher's Hollow for one of its early residents, Eli Beecher. A portion of the town now lies under the Sacandaga. Once a covered bridge connected Edinburg with Batchellerville.

The signs on Edinburg's newer structures speak for themselves. Burt's Diner welcomes hunters with a promised opening of 4 AM. It is closed. However, you can buy "Groceries and Stuff" at Fullers Corner convenience store. And the newer church across the street tells you the time of day with the words JESUS SAVES replacing numerals. Past, present and future mix comfortably in Edinburg.

There's something about early spring that brings out the stick-poking in kids. Just check the two boys working on the run-off near Batchellerville bridge. Already they've got a good stream going.

Once Batchellerville was a thriving community of some 500 people and included grocery stores, a school, churches, and a factory for the manufacture of woodenware. It was named for the Batcheller brothers who had built a mill on this site.

Nearly everything has changed about Batchellerville except its name. Much of the original community is now under water. The Presbyterian Church still stands. A few cars are parked in front of the

restaurant/bar at the corner. A sign marks the location of the Town of Edinburg park. Near the site of the old covered bridge, a side road pushes over the hill to Lake Desolation.

The road south passes another picnic area overlooking the bridge, and the landmark I-Go-Inn. Nearby, a small stream cascades hillside rocks on its way to the lake. According to the map, Fish House should be nearby.

"It's just over the hill," said the man at the country store.

"But don't turn right at the crossroads," chimed in a customer. "That road's a little wet these days."

I soon discovered what he meant. The road which went to the right abruptly stopped at water's edge. The historical marker nearby reported Fish House's covered bridge was torn down in 1930. But old-timers claim the townspeople had hoped to save it. Unfortunately, when high winds and rough waters snapped one of the steel cables they had attached, the bridge slipped off its foundation and settled to the bottom of the new lake. Today, where the road drops into the water, is a sign: BOAT LAUNCH + OR PARKING $4.00.

The old village square also lies somewhere under Sacandaga's breaking cover of ice. The Shew House, dating from 1784 still stands, as does another brick structure on the corner. Sir William Johnson would hardly recognize the site he picked in 1762 for his fishing and hunting lodge.

The mix of camps, houses and mobile homes continues through the Benedict area. The Hudson River-Black River Regulating District is the dominant political body in this region—controlling the release of water to downstream businesses and communities, and setting many of the ground rules for recreational use of the lake. Not surprising, the Regulating District and camp owners are often at odds.

North Broadalbin is little more than a bend in the road. The Hemlock Church is here. So is the North Broadalbin Beach Club. Duncan McMartin once operated a mill at the mouth of Frenchmen's Creek. Today children fish the stream.

At Riceville, a boy walks the road with a bamboo pole on his shoulder. There's time for bullheading before Riceville's fields are dry enough to plant.

When Route 30 was routed around Mayfield, a new business district sprung up along the highway. Now you can buy leather goods, snowshoes, antiques, or find a place to eat, sleep or mail a letter without even turning off the road. Downtown Mayfield is not what it used to be.

Today more bikes than cars are parked at the Convenient Corner. It's Saturday and the Rhubard Foodery is closed. So is the Coleco factory.

But up the street there's plenty of activity. Workers are removing the charred remains and debris from what had been an apartment house. The ladies of the Central Presbyterian Church are getting ready for a Spaghetti Supper, and in the church yard the kids are boomeranging.

"Can you throw this thing so it'll come back? " asked one of the kids.

"Like Crocodile Dundee," I replied, whipping the curved stick toward open yard. Suddenly it swerved onto a collision course with one of the Spaghetti Supper ladies. I shouted. She ducked. The boomerang zoomed briefly upward and dropped harmlessly to ground.

"Whew!"

"Maybe he's better with a Frisbee," said one of the kids.

"No way!"

From across the yard, the Spaghetti Supper lady managed a smile.

Years ago, Cranberry Creek had a population of several hundred, and the women in town made gloves at home for the factories to the south. Now a church and a handful of houses remain. But this is a day you don't dwell on the past—not when you can play catch in a sideyard, relax on the porch—or cut up a tree. Maybe dream about the walleyes that fill the creek bank-to-bank during the spawning run.

"I'd rather be fishing," said the man standing over a huge maple which was down but not out. "Just want to get it into small enough hunks to haul away. Then I'll get fishing again."

Right now the Sacandaga is filled to the brim— protecting downstream communities from flooding. During the dry summer months the lake gradually is lowered, often too much in the eyes of the businesses and camp owners. With each summer release, the friction between the Regulating District and area interests increases, especially as the local economy grows more and more dependent on tourism.

Tourism is hardly new to Sacandaga Park. Developed by the Fonda, Johnstown and Gloversville Railroad in the 1870's, this 75-acre resort along the Sacandaga River quickly became the major recreation center for the region. Inns, cottages, a theater and golf course were all here. Its most renowned attraction was Sport Island—a unique development where several famous athletic exhibitions were held. Sport Island, as well as the roadbed for the train, are now under water.

Sacandaga's golf course remains, and on this April day, players are out for their first match of the year. Some of the original cottages are still here, too. Already, a few have opened for the season—continuing a century-old tradition.

These old places along the Sacandaga are like Noah's Ark: somehow they survived the flood.

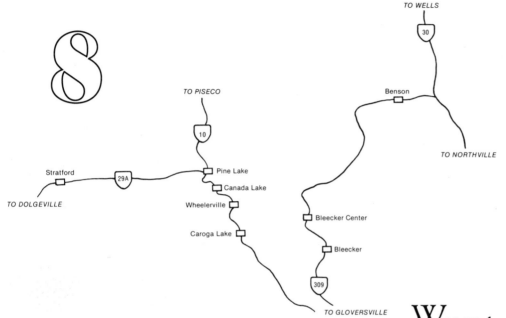

8

TO WELLS

30

Benson

TO NORTHVILLE

TO PISECO

10

Stratford

29A

Pine Lake

Canada Lake

Wheelerville

TO DOLGEVILLE

Caroga Lake

Bleecker Center

Bleecker

309

TO GLOVERSVILLE

BENSON
BLEECKER
CAROGA LAKE
WHEELERVILLE
CANADA LAKE
PINE LAKE
STRATFORD

WHAT do you call the road which wiggles through the Town of Benson? Is it Route 6, as one map says? Or Route 125, as another claims? A third map plays it safe—assigning no route number. Ordinarily, a mix-up like this could trigger an identity crisis.

But when you're talking about the road where most of Benson lives, it doesn't much matter what you call it.

Around here, roots are more important than routes. People simply call their highway Benson Road. This is the road to anywhere from Benson. It's also the only paved road through town.

Those who live here know every rise and dip in their road, each bump and patch. They also know about the "pothole" law the town passed a while back....the one which requires advance written notification of a road hazard before a damage claim involving that hazard can be filed. Apparently, a person's first trip across Benson is officially viewed as a scouting expedition.

Driving along Benson's road, one gets the feeling a new trail is about to be blazed. But winter has left few scars this year, and the ride over the ridge is quite smooth. Obviously, the frost heaves have settled and this year's crop of potholes already are patched. The town highway department has done its job.

This day is bright, cold. Smoke rises from a chimney of a roadside dwelling. Winter may be past, but not the heating season. Just off the road, three hikers huddle around a large boulder which serves as their picnic table. From a tree above, a crow sounds Benson's noon whistle.

Next to the town hall are signposts marking the trail north to

79

Cathead Mountain and westward to the Northville-Lake Placid trail. There's little need for conventional road markers in Benson. Much of the town lies within the Silver Lake Wilderness Area where motorized vehicles are not allowed.

More and more people are discovering Benson's rugged beauty. Its population grew from 89 in 1970 to 156 in 1980—an increase of over 75%. Even so, the town has neither gas station nor grocery store. But it does have an outstanding cross-country ski area at Lapland Lake operated by a former Olympic skier.

How does a town with a population of 156 meet its needs? Some services Benson itself provides; others are purchased from nearby towns. The HAMILTON COUNTY NEWS reported contracts in a recent year with Northampton for ambulance service ($500), and Hope for dog warden service ($200). The paper also reported the appointment of town residents to several volunteer committees including those for town dinners, and deer feeding. Sooner or later, you get to meet all your neighbors in Benson.

The hilly, wooded terrain continues into the Town of Bleecker, past an abandoned farmhouse with the remains of a stone fence to the turnoff for the Adirondack Beagle Hare Club. Just about every corner in Bleecker has a name. Lindsley Corners, Peters Corners, Bowlers Corners are all here. Pinnacle is nearby, too, where Tannery Road joins. But for some reason Pinnacle was not caught in a Corner.

At Bleecker Center, the road bends abruptly southward, passing the farm where a boy holds a fluttering kite. Quickly, the kite soars up and away—beyond barn and tree.

"Look Mom! Look Mom!" he shouted to the woman hanging wash in the yard. The boy's mother watched as the kite dipped and climbed high above the power lines.

A car stopped up the road while its driver, too, viewed this rite of spring.

The sign above the entrance of Bleecker's Town Hall is neatly lettered in Old English. Nearby is Parish Road which leads to the shrine of the first Catholic Church in Fulton County. Soon the road makes a sharp turn around Tumble Inn and out of the Park.

This time of year, there's no telling what Caroga Lake's amusement park is like. Who knows how far you can see from atop the Ferris wheel? Or what plinky tunes the merry-go-round might play to the delight of summer's children? For now, rides are stilled, and a chilling wind blows off the lake. Caroga still hibernates—its stores, cottages and state park awaiting the season of fun.

No one should be surprised that Ungers fails to make most maps.

There's not much to Ungers. But Wheelerville sometimes is overlooked as well. The Town of Caroga Municipal Offices, Town Justice Court and Wheelerville Union Free School are all in Wheelerville. So is the Nick Stoner Inn and the Nick Stoner Municipal Golf Course, complete with a stern-faced statue of Major Nicholas Stoner and his rifle overlooking a fairway. Nick helps keep scorecards honest, some say. Any place with a statue to its hero should make the map.

After laboring up the hill overlooking Canada Lake, the car is rewarded with a gentle coast past Green Lake and on to the Canada Lake Store/Post Office.

"I hear they're already biting on Ontario," said a woman.

"Maybe I'll go there next weekend," replied the man checking out a six-pack. "Too cold to even wet a line here."

"Guess we're beating the season a little," added his companion. "They're still ice fishing on Indian Lake, you know."

Pine Lake is a bend in the road with a barn and two signs, one pointing to the Pine Lake campground and the other proclaiming ADIRONDACK PARADISE.

Nearing Stratford, woods give way to pasture and cornfield. Soon a farmhouse appears. The ground is still cold and wet—weeks away from plowing, and weeks more until planting.

82

Houses line the street across from the Stratford School. Both the post office and general store at the bottom of the hill are closed. On a side street are the charred remains of what had been a house. Only its block chimney stands. The first tannery in Stratford was erected just across East Canada Creek in 1812. Nearby are several of the town's older buildings including the Baptist and Methodist Churches.

A sign at the edge of town says "LEAVING ADIRONDACK PARK." In the field beyond, deer cautiously graze—their bodies thin from winter. Man is not alone in welcoming warmer days.

"Man is not alone in welcoming warmer days."

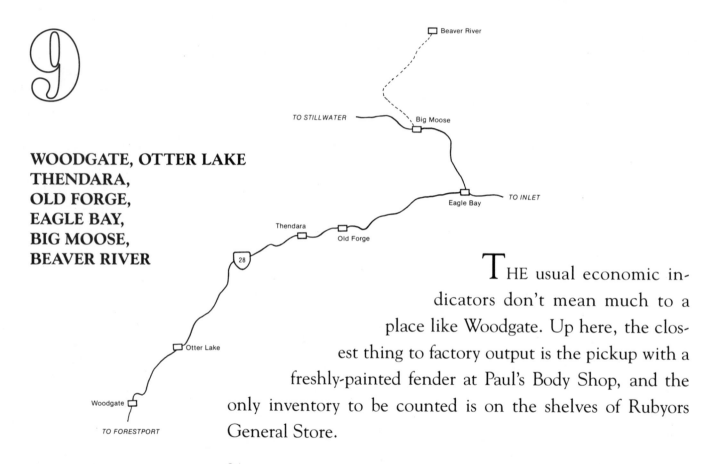

9

WOODGATE, OTTER LAKE
THENDARA,
OLD FORGE,
EAGLE BAY,
BIG MOOSE,
BEAVER RIVER

THE usual economic in-
dicators don't mean much to a
place like Woodgate. Up here, the clos-
est thing to factory output is the pickup with a
freshly-painted fender at Paul's Body Shop, and the
only inventory to be counted is on the shelves of Rubyors
General Store.

84

So you look for other ways to check on Woodgate's commerce. Things like the number of bags dropped off at the post office in Rubyors, or the number of notices on the bulletin board. Today, the mailman dropped off three partially-filled sacks. The bags should get fatter once the summer people start coming to Little Long Lake and White Lake.

Woodgate's bulletin board is already at 100% capacity. It's packed with thumbtacked ads and posters of things for sale, services available. You can buy firewood ready to burn, or a woodlot ready to cut. Two cars are for sale. They both "run good." So does the used snowmobile which "goes for the first $700." And LOU'S ELECTRIC SERVICE promises "QUALITY WORK AT HONEST PRICES!" Who could ask for anything more?

Perhaps car counting is the most accurate check of business during the summer. You just sit on the porch on a Friday night and count the cars headed north. Amazing how well one can predict the weekend business at Old Forge or Inlet while enjoying a gentle breeze and a cool soda.

Otter Lake has a few stores and eating places catering to passing tourists. It also has a fire hall and two churches, including St. Mary's of the Snow. At a nearby house, two kids are playing catch.

Spring also is in the air at the Otter Lake General Store. A sign above the entrance identifies SAM DRUCKER'S STORE.

85

"That TV show goes back a few years," I remarked to the proprietor, who was considerably younger than the Sam Drucker I recalled.

"Amazing the number who call me Sam," he replied. "But older people…they know the difference between Otter Lake and Hooterville."

This is the season the FOR SALE signs start sprouting along the road. On cars, boats, trailers, camps, trees—just about anything. The woods becomes one gigantic flea market in the spring. or is it fly market? At least, that's the way it used to be.

These days, however, more and more towns are treating the streams with an inoculant called BTI to destroy the black fly larvae. Still no one claims the black flies have become an endangered species—not yet anyway. But people seem to be taking fewer swipes at the air during May and June.

Not far from McKeever, a state marker designates the site of a forest fire early in the century. New growth has long since erased the scar. Nearby, logs are piled high at the section of the old state road used as a loading area for this new harvest.

Grass grows high on the tracks of the Adirondack Railway at Thendara. The years, too, have taken their toll on the work cars which stand idle on the siding—paint peeling, wheels rusting. However, the passenger car resting nearby appears ready to roll even now…awaiting

86

only the conductor's call of "ALL ABOARD!....for Carter Station...Big Moose....Bee-ver River!" But today no engine steams, no whistle sounds. No passengers scurry from Thendara House, or Vanauken's tavern to make the train.

Thendara's new business area has developed along Route 28, including the Steak House Restaurant, Uncle Sam's Fabric Center, and an attractive mini-mall with shops, offices and post office. It has about everything—except a train.

Crossing the bridge, Old Forge quickly shows its tourist image. Motels, gas stations, restaurants and gift shops are everywhere. But further along, homes replace commerce, and Old Forge becomes a pleasant mountain community.

The schoolyard is empty this week of Spring Break, except for the boy on his bike and the girl who pushes a baby carriage along the school walk. She laughs nervously as he jokes with her. Suddenly the wind picks up and the wash in a nearby yard blows every which way. Last fall's leaves swirl in from a neighbor's yard, and a rubber tire swings from a limb.

Down the street, an elderly woman still layered for winter greets a friend sweeping her porch.

"Don't you know it's 64 today?" said the woman on the porch. "You're walking around like it's zero."

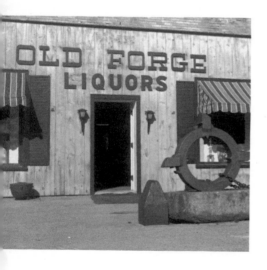

"I don't put this coat away until the wind dies down," replied her friend. "That'll be May, I bet."

These are bonus days in Old Forge, a time for friends to joke about the weather and stroll the streets. Before they fill with strange faces from Utica, Syracuse, and points south.

In the early 19th century, there was a forge here. Unfortunately, the ore in this area proved to be of low grade, and the new forge soon became an abandoned old forge. But the settlement which survived had found its name. Today, three pieces of the original forge are mounted in front of the Old Forge Liquor Store—a tribute to the community's namesake.

Across the street, Old Forge Hardware promotes its "Mud Season" Sale, with 40% off the red tag items. People say if you can't find what you're looking for at Old Forge Hardware, they don't make it. They're probably right.

The marquee of the theater says "HAPPY BIG 25 JACK AND BARB." Now there's a show that's been playing a long time. Over at Enchanted Forest, two men roll up the plastic covering which had protected an outdoor exhibit last winter.

Across the lake, a mother and child walk an empty beach. Impulsively, the child runs to water's edge and tosses a pebble into the water. Quickly, mother retrieved her child, then tosses a stone of her own—ringing the calm of First Lake.

Nearing Eagle Bay, a boy with fishing rod in hand walks the road. He paused to greet the tanned oldster raking his yard. Further along, a young mother pushes a baby carriage across the street from Friendly Market. It's the supper hour—a relaxed time of day around Eagle Bay. But just wait until Saturday night! Bet the Hard Times Cafe will be bouncing then.

Better slow down when you turn onto Big Moose Road…and tighten your seat belt, too. The road is one big bump. After all, you don't want to miss the deer grazing in the yard at the log cabin, or the hawk circling above.

Ice still floats on Big Moose. At day's end, calm water reflects boathouse and hillside on the opposite shore. This moment belongs to the sparrow—or is it a chickadee?—chirping high in the pine behind the chapel.

It was nearby in South Bay where Chester Gilette many years before turned a holiday with Grace Brown into a deliberate drowning—thus setting the stage for what Theodore Dreiser termed "An American Tragedy." Now, a second American Tragedy has befallen the lake. Big Moose runs clear and lifeless, the victim of acid rain.

A hand-painted sign at the intersection points the way to Big Moose hamlet. Bumping along, there's evidence the highway department already has made its spring inspection—staking red markers at a section of washed-out shoulder. Winter has left its mark on the caved-in building across the tracks, too. But optimism knows no bounds in Big Moose. Already someone has painted HANDYMAN'S DREAM above the FOR SALE signs on its crumbling side.

These days, the Big Moose train station offers GAS, COFFEE, HOT DOGS, THINGS. But it is closed, and the street is empty, too—except for a dog which responded with a wag to my command of "Sit!" Together we embarked on a tour of Big Moose...past the camps decorated with old bottles, deer horns, and a bent airplane prop...beyond the asphalt-sided Catholic Church...all the way to the barricade across the road to Stillwater. Obviously, this is not a road to take during mud season.

At least there's a road to Stillwater. Nothing goes to Beaver River—except rusting tracks. In the days the train came through, a road wasn't all that important. But Beaver River is on its own now the train is gone...awaiting the time a road might come its way. Meanwhile, there's the Volkswagon.

It must have been a happy day when someone discovered his Volkswagon fit perfectly on the aging tracks. So the enterprising folks at

Beaver River simply welded circular steel plates to the inside of the wheels to keep their new-found train on the iron trail to Big Moose.

The ride goes slowly, I'm told, as the track isn't in good shape. And there's no turnaround in Big Moose, either. So you shift into reverse for the return trip, and back up the five miles. Which could make for a stiff neck if you insist on looking in the direction you're moving. But then, the other choice is a five-mile hike—which could make for sore feet.

When snow piles high, the Volkswagon gets a rest. Then snowmobilers run the tracks to the Beaver River Hotel. In other seasons, fishermen and hunters sometimes come by boat. Beaver River welcomes everyone, however they arrive. Someday perhaps by car—one that's a road runner.

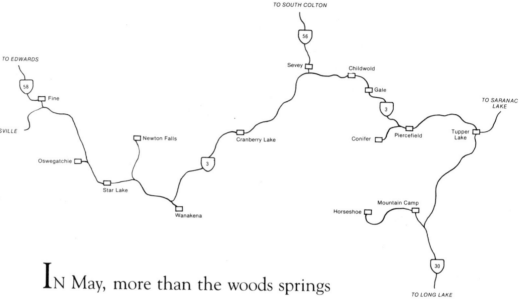

HORSESHOE
MOUNTAIN CAMP
TUPPER LAKE
PIERCEFIELD
CONIFER
GALE
CHILDWOLD
SEVEY
CRANBERRY LAKE
WANAKENA
NEWTON FALLS
STAR LAKE
OSWEGATCHIE
FINE

IN May, more than the woods springs to life. Just about everyone in the Adirondacks banks on THE SEASON…that brief period between Memorial Day and Labor Day when downstaters invade with tents, trailers, boats—and dollars.

Preparations have been underway for weeks. Town crews are fixing roads, cutting brush, zapping black fly larvae. State campgrounds are opening. Seasonal motel and restaurant operators are back from Florida, patching, painting, perking up. This is the season to plant flower boxes along Main Street and plan the church and fire department fund raisers. Hope runs high in May.

By month's end, all is ready for summer's dress rehearsal. But Memorial Weekend makes its entry with a raw wind from the north. Dark skies threaten rain—perhaps snow. This dress rehearsal might call for an overcoat before the curtain drops.

Still, trailers ply the mountain roads, and hardy souls pitch tent and tarp at Horseshoe Lake a few miles south of Tupper Lake. Once wood is gathered and fire started, it's time to fish a nearby stream. The parka-clad camper smiles as her bobbin dips. Even a menacing weekend has its advantage. No crowds. No black flies. Just hungry bullheads.

Further along, the road to Horseshoe turns to gravel, then ends abruptly. Once Horseshoe was a lively station on the Adirondack Railway. Now the road reverts to trail as wilderness recalls its loan.

These days Mountain Camp is unoccupied and the road leading to the veterans' facility barricaded. Perhaps another road is open, but I settled for a peek at the buildings across South Bay from Bog River bridge. Here a fisherman tries his luck at the foot of the falls. The day is almost too windy for fishing.

The streets of Tupper Lake show little evidence a holiday weekend is underway. Some townspeople don't mind. They're content to watch a loader as it digs out the debris of a demolished building on Main Street.

"Doesn't take long to tear a place down," said one of the onlookers.

"Sure quicker than putting it up," echoes another. "Won't even know what was there by the end of the day."

The little boy tugged his Mother's arm. "Hey Mom, what was there?"

Two women sort through a sidewalk sale up the street while their husbands wait nearby—patient for the moment. A teenager stops at the vacant Newberrys just long enough to eye the strangers, then pedals up the hill toward Sunmount. Not much excitement except for the demolition.

Downtown may have seen better days, but it's fighting back. The campaign for a new Civic Center is well along, according to the progress thermometer on the side of the FREE PRESS building. Main Street is being landscaped, buildings spruced up.

A sign at the Municipal Park promotes Woodsmen's Days in July. But this day is for softball; a spirited game already is underway, and another team warms up in the park. Across the street, cars splash through

94

puddles of a recent rain. The A & P Supermarket, Ames Department Store, McDonalds, and several other businesses are here. Route 3 is Tupper's newest center of commerce—the latest chapter in its colorful history.

Soon after the railroad came to Tupper Lake, sawmills and wood-product factories appeared overnight. So did the lumberjacks, down from the woods for supplies and a good time. This was their town...friendly, spirited, slightly rough edged. Tupper Lake still makes no pretenses. What you see is what you get: a mountain community rich in tradition—again in transition.

French Canadians first worked the woods and settled this area. Why would Faust, the community which developed along the railroad, carry a name rooted in German legend? An academic question, for when Tupper Lake's new post office was built, the one in Faust was closed. Without a postmark of its own, Faust again became legend.

"Only two factories left," said the shopkeeper. "Hardwood veneer, and plastics. That's a far cry from the old days."

"Still got the train station, too," chimed in a customer. "Now all we need is the train!"

Piercefield was originally a company town, but today the community is on its own. Even Route 3 has bypassed it, leaving the old state

road and most of Piercefield behind. No traffic problem here. When you go to the Town Hall, you're also at the Highway Department, Medical Center, Youth Center, Board Room, and Court Room. They're all in the same building.

The former church down the street lacks a steeple, and the bell is now mounted on a short pedestal in the churchyard. Still the old building serves. BINGO SUNDAYS 8:00 P.M., says a sign nailed to a nearby maple.

Piercefield is a community of small houses, front porches, stone fences. Recent rains have brought lilacs to bloom, dandelions to seed. Now grass grows high. But these are not lawns you mow every time it rains.

The trees along the road to Conifer are deciduous. In the early years of the century, Conifer was a thriving community with company store, hotel, and a sawmill which operated day and night. All are gone. Only a few closely-spaced houses remain. The forest creeps ever closer.

Back on Route 3, the Boy Scout Camp and cemetery of Gale quickly pass. Now drizzle turns to downpour. A woman continues to hang her wash.

Childwold is dressed for company. A gift shop displays its selection of baskets. The restaurant, motel and leather shop are open, too. Cars are few today. Childwold's company arrives when school is out.

A small roadsign marks Sevey at the intersection of Route 56. Sevey's Windfall House has a sign, too. But the message is faded—its business gone. Headstones in the cemetery carry the name of this pioneer family as well. But change is in the air. A sign at one house now calls the place HARDSHIP CORNERS. Wonder if the Seveys would object to a new name for their settlement?

Fishing is still the thing to do on Cranberry Lake, but these days there are more excuses than catches.

"Sure not what it used to be," said the old-timer at Cranberry Lake Inn. "Some people say rain like this messes up the lake. Only thing I know is they're not there...or they're not biting. Either way I don't catch 'em."

Now the playful wind turns angry, and a boat bangs against the dock at Emporium Marine. No day to be on the lake. Much better to catch up on town news...maybe put in a load at the laundromat...pick up some groceries at the IGA.

True to its name, Ranger School Road leads to the Wanakena campus of the State School of Environmental Science and Forestry. School's already out, and the last students today leave their classroom at the edge of the wilderness. Here some of the nation's top rangers have been trained, and some of the nation's lowest temperatures recorded.

A large sawblade serves as Wanakena's welcome sign, an appropriate greeting for this hamlet carved from woods. Summer cottages blend with year-round homes and a general store—united by a footbridge suspended across the Oswegatchie.

Newton Falls is one of few company towns thriving in the Adirondacks. The papermill still is king, the community its grateful subject. Homes are inviting, lawns trim, gardens planted. The hotel dating from the porch age still stands square, All's well in Newton Falls, even when the flag flies wildly and churchgoers splash their way to St. Anthony's.

Wind whips the flag at Star Lake's golf course, too—open for the season, but closed for the day. An old building with the date 1892 sculpted above its door is hosting a community meeting. A few cars are parked at the Star Lake Hotel, no doubt for a different meeting.

Now rain stops and wind retreats. Rolling pastures replace wooded hills, and farms appear. Oswegatchie's cemetery may be more populated than the quiet hamlet off Route 3 where a group of boys pause at the bridge to view the stranger.

"What are you taking a picture of?" yelled the boldest.

"The deer horns and the old car," I replied.

Satisfied, Oswegatchie's welcoming committee moved on—past the Baptist Church and around the bend.

Not far from Fine, a huge lilac blooms where once a farmstead stood. Today, only an overgrown stone foundation remains...man's handiwork already forgotten. But the old church still stands—its cross slightly tipped—at the edge of the field.

11

PORTERS CORNERS
FOWLERVILLE
BRANTINGHAM
SPERRYVILLE
NUMBER FOUR
STILLWATER

SOMETIMES a humid June day turns angry without warning. Suddenly, the sky above Moose River Road darkens, then rain and wind erupt...sending whirligigs to frenzy, children and Mother to cover. The little porch fills with wet kids and their dog, Mom and her basket of unhung wash.

100

Briefly, Mother and children share the pleasure of a cooling rain...playing catch with the big drops splattering from the rail...laughing at the tire swinging wildly from the big maple...screeching when the dog shakes dry. Then wind and rain retreat. June's prodigal sun returns. This storm did the peonies no favor, and the big maple gave up a limb. But not the limb that holds the tire. Soon the kids are back on their swing, and Mother returns to her clothesline. It's business as usual along the Moose River.

A Niagara Mohawk crew already is at Porters Corners on the western edge of the Park, repairing lines downed by the storm. Quickly service is returned to the log cabin and other homes in the area, and the truck is on its way.

Old-timers talk of logging runs on the Big Moose and the pioneer settlement of French lumberjacks nearby. Now a pulp truck rolls down the road to the mill in Lyons Falls, passing the simple shrine honoring St. Anthony and the Church which served this early logging community.

Direction and caution signs along the road are peppered with shots, especially those which show a bouncing deer. But hunters around here are not after angora rabbits. That hand-crafted sign remains intact.

Fowlerville is just up the hill from Moose River bridge. The intersection includes a camp, an open field, and two houses.

In the country, you greet a stranger with your eyes—up and down. Sometimes you talk; sometimes you don't. Depends on what you see. The man stopped the lawn mower. A good sign.

"What you doing over this way? Aren't lost, are you?"

Bet the only time a stranger stops in Fowlerville is to ask directions.

"I was hoping for a road sign."

That brought a laugh.

"Not enough traffic for signs. Mostly the rafters, and the little boats that bob around."

We talked about the old days when there had been a logging camp down the road and people would walk all over the woods— even across Moose River Plains to Perkins Clearing, a jaunt of some 50 miles.

"We'd walk that far just to fish. But the catch was worth it," said the man, smiling.

He told me about a bull moose that had joined a herd of cows over in Highmarket. Finally the farmer had to call the conservation people to move it out.

"Would you believe…it headed right back to Tug Hill?"

Guess that moose had an eye for one of those heifers.

"Have you seen moose tracks around here?" I asked.

"Not just tracks but trails, too. They plow through the small stuff like a bulldozer."

"Have you seen one?"

"Not yet. But when I go in the woods I bring my camera. One of these days I'll get a picture."

Bet he will. After all, he's living next to the Moose River.

The road beyond Fowlerville was more logging trail than highway. No buildings, no power lines, no road signs. The man said there wasn't much. He was right, and so were his directions. Finally, another road...then across Fish Creek and up to Brantingham. I couldn't find the way again if I wanted.

Now Fowlerville seemed a world removed, even if it was only six miles to the WELCOME display the Brantingham Community Association had erected. Suddenly, I was in the suburbs, or so it felt...with a restaurant called Coach Light Inn...a General Store featuring miniature golf...a lake more suited to party boats than fishing boats...and friendly people who wave welcome with glass in hand. Brantingham looks tame, busy, social. A place you'd likely find mousse—not moose.

Brantingham's golf course is in the swing, too. A few sports are on the course, but more are at the clubhouse. Suddenly skies again darkened. Time to leave this woodland suburb before the next downpour.

Radio Boonville sounded a thunderstorm alert. But nothing happened and soon the sun returned. The radio patter continues along the road to Sperryville. It's June Dairy month, and the announcer reminds me to send in my name and phone number. "Then.. when we call you, just give us your best MOO...and YOU can be eligible to compete in the big MOO-OFF at the Lewis County Fair."

"Moo-oo, Moo-oo," I practiced, sounding pretty good along the road to Sperryville. But what would I do with the registered holstein calf they're giving as a prize? Maybe I could get that moose to visit.

"Is this Sperryville?" I asked the kids pushing bikes up the hill.

"It's at the corner with the sign," replied the tall boy. "Can't miss it."

The corner I found had two houses, and a mobile home further along. Sure enough, just off the road and hidden by brush was Sperryville's own sign. Then abruptly the road ended, with nothing but woods beyond. Like it or not, you live on the edge in Sperryville.

Number Four was a forest outpost when its hotel was built in 1826. Now the hotel is gone, and the road extends to Stillwater. A few hunting camps are here, and there's a place called The Trading Post where you can get camping and fishing supplies. But not much else has changed. Number Four is still a forest outpost.

Of course, there's a bar where you can buy a tee shirt or a can of maple syrup—but that's for tourists. Also you can play a game of pool.

"Me and Ma are going to break, aren't we Ma?" said the girl to her beer-drinking Mother.

"You don't mind if we break, do you?" said Mother to the woman behind the bar.

"A rack of balls is the only thing you can break around here without buying it," chuckled the woman.

The sign at Stillwater Inn declares here's WHERE THE ROAD ENDS AND THE GOOD TIMES BEGIN. But most who come this way park at the boat launch and have their good times fishing the reservoir. Except the busload of kids who head straight for ice cream at The Stillwater Shop.

The hard-packed road continues on to Big Moose. Today there is no traffic, no fishermen at the bridge. Just Radio Boonville promoting its GREAT MOO-OFF...and a girl singing: "Boys like you give love a bad name...."

When you're on the back road to Big Moose, it's easy to flick the switch on civilization. "Click"...and gone are the unlikely lyrics—just like that! Now silence...except for the chatter of a red squirrel high in a pine. Out here, that's music enough.

"when you're on the back road to Big Moose, it's easy to flick the switch on civilization."

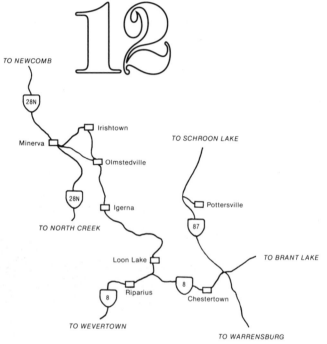

12

**MINERVA, IRISHTOWN,
OLMSTEDVILLE, IGERNA,
LOON LAKE, RIPARIUS,
CHESTERTOWN, POTTERSVILLE**

THE stretch of Route 28N south of the High Peaks is remembered not for its scenic views—though some are outstanding—but for an historic nighttime journey nearly a century ago.

Vice President Theodore Roosevelt had been hiking in the High Peaks when word was received that President McKinley, victim of an assassin's bullet, had taken a turn for the worse. The Roosevelt party quickly boarded a horse-drawn wagon for the arduous ride to their train at North Creek. As they raced into the Town of Minerva, death came to the stricken President.

Town residents were asleep that September night in 1901, unaware of the drama unfolding in their backyard. Still, this was not the first time Minerva found itself in the spotlight. Winslow Homer, who summered at the North Woods Club, had captured the area's unspoiled beauty on canvas. Too, the town had received widespread recognition during the campaign waged by Assemblyman Wesley Barnes on behalf of the original Forest Preserve Act. For his dedication, this son of Minerva was honored with the title "Keeper of the Forest." In the Adirondacks, that's as close as one gets to knighthood.

"Are you coming to Discover Minerva Day?" asked the young man arranging a craft display at the corner.

I glanced up and down the street, wondering what there was to discover. A woman was pushing a baby carriage in the direction of Murdie's General Store. Two men were passing the time of day in front of the post office. A pickup kicked dust on its way out of the town hall.

"We just want to let people know the town's still on the map," explained the young man.

"Are you one of the old families?" I asked.

He laughed. "We're imports...and soon will be exports. Last winter was just too cold. Going to California."

Some families come here for 150 years—and some for 150 days.

At Minerva's town park, the happy sounds of children on an outing echo over the waters of an unspoiled lake rimmed in balsam and pine. This place is about as far from the cares of the world as you can get—even when you're not a kid. Here's something worth discovering in Minerva.

Longs Hill Road crosses a small bridge leading to a neatly painted country church surrounded by headstones. Built in the mid-nineteenth century, St. Mary's of Irishtown wears its years well. These days there's little else to Irishtown except the playing field for Minerva's Little League.

An old stone wall peeks through trees along the road to Olmstedville. Water rolls over the log dam where William Hill had built a gristmill early in the 1800s. Now ducks play in the water, sliding down the slippery spillway like kids. Nearby is a rowboat and a picnic table. The old millpond is good for people, too.

A logging truck chugs over the narrow bridge, leading a procession of cars and travel trailers headed into the woods. This is the season most choose to explore the winding mountain roads.

Maybe more visitors will be stopping at Olmstedville this year. On the corner where a carpentry shop had piled dust a year before is an attractive gift shop, complete with folding Adirondack chairs and whimsical deer fashioned from a birch tree.

Olmstedville is ready for Discover Minerva Day. Petunias, marigold and impatiens fill a large wood planter in front of the shop. Board and Batten Antiques has spruced up for the occasion, and the Minerva Historical Society has planted annuals in the old guide boat. The whole town will be in bloom for the celebration.

Over at the Country Diner they're talking about another event— the school Regents.

"Which test does she take today?" asked the woman in a print dress.

"Math…I think," said her companion. "Or is it chemistry? I get 'em all mixed up."

"Whew! I never could get either one."

She looked over at the salesman in the corner. But he wasn't thinking school. Just how many calls he had ahead of him this afternoon before heading back to the Northway.

"Don't forget our Olympic skier," called the waitress as he left.

The salesman dropped a coin into a ski boot near the door to help an area youngster train for a spot on the Olympic Ski Team.

"I won't say 'break a leg'," he called back.

True to its name, Church Road led past the North Chester Baptist Church. Then a downhill plunge, and the map said I was on North Gore Road. Interesting. Next the few houses of Byrnes Corners and Hardscrabble Road. I'm changing roads without even turning. Another sprinkling of houses. Igerna perhaps? Sure enough, the map changed names again. Thank goodness, Igerna Road took me onto Route 9. For all its aliases, my shortcut was quite direct. It was only the name changes that kept me spinning.

The motels at Loon Lake are open, flowers are blooming and pool furniture is out. Across the lake, a seaplane bobs in the breeze, and an outboard circles the bay. At the beach, a boy bellysplashes off the raft. Girls screech. Not to be outdone, another boy jumps in—feet first, arms flailing. Loon Lake already is awash with the fun of summer.

Back when free enterprise was involved in the operation of turnpikes and bridges, a trip across the Hudson River at Riparius was said to cost a nickel for a horse and its rider, ten cents if the horse was pulling a rig, fifteen cents when a team was used, and thirty cents if the crossing was made by stage. Wonder what that pulp truck rolling down the hill and across the steel bridge would pay? If tolls were still collected on a graduated scale, its driver would have to dig deep.

Times also have changed for the settlement which developed

around the bridge. Years ago it was called Riverside. Unfortunately, there was another Riverside in the state, and the postal service decided that Riverside on the Hudson had to find a new name. So its name was changed to the Latin equivalent of Riverside. This was the dawning of the age of Riparius—to paraphrase a rock song of the era.

But not many people in Riparius speak Latin. So Riverside it remains, in the hearts if not the postmarks of the community. There's still a Riverside Oil Company, and the Riverside Station Road follows the tracks into town past the Riverside Volunteer Fire Department.

I wonder what sort of river borders the other Riverside? Could the kids there put inner tubes in their river and float downstream to heart's content? That's what the kids here are doing today…racing the clouds, and the little dog chasing along the shore. Can the kids in the other Riverside do this?

The Town of Chester found itself on the map early in the 19th century when it became the southern terminus for a road extending northwesterly to Russell in St. Lawrence County. These early roads were little more than trails. The years may have erased too much to tell exactly where Chester's first road ran.

These days Chestertown has no lack of roads. Routes 8 and 9 pass through, and Exit 25 of the Northway is just to the east of the hamlet.

The Greyhound stops here. But today only the driver stepped off. Soon the bus was on its way, Chestertown's population unchanged.

The man and woman who had viewed the arrival and departure of no one now turned their attention to the window of Janser's Drug Store, and the display of cabbage patch dolls at a picnic. The biker huffing up the hill turned his attention to Bill and Amy's A.B.C. Coffee Shop.

"Does A.B.C. stand for Amy and Bill's Coffee?" he asked.

"Hey … that's not bad," said a man seated next to him. "I thought it meant you'd get your order as easy as ABC. Maybe it means both."

One sign behind the counter said NO OUT OF TOWN CHECKS CASHED. Beneath it, perhaps as an afterthought, was further qualification: NO PERSONAL CHECKS CASHED. Everyone knows you don't do your banking at Bill and Amy's.

Now and then, people here are reminded they live on the edge of the woods. One summer night not long ago, a huge black bear gave territorial notice to a resident by climbing through an open window—holding the frightened man hostage in his own bedroom for over an hour. The visit was duly noted in the Glens Falls paper.

And students at North Hudson Central in Chestertown had an unexpected day off when water from a nearby beaver pond backed up through the school's sewers. The beavers were live-trapped and moved to

112

a new home back in the woods. The next day it was school as usual. Of course the kids are hoping their furry friends will return. There's nothing like having a "beaver day" now and then.

What's happened to Pottersville, I wondered? No one was around this afternoon. No cars at the post office or the Corner Hardware. Even the Black Bear Restaurant was closed. Besides, the cutout of a mean bear on its door didn't exactly say "Welcome stranger."

Then a pulp truck rounded the corner sputtering black smoke. Slowly the town awoke. Two boys on bikes appeared. Then a girl with a clarinet case. Moments later, a motorcycle pulled into the Wells House. Any minute the stage could arrive. Wells House looks like something out of a Western.

Up the street, the antique shop is ready for the season. The place is packed with memorabilia and collectibles—including the bookcase and school marm's desk from the old school in Riverside.

"They're converting the school to a house," I reported.

"I haven't been to Riverside in some time," said the woman.

"Hi Gram," yelled a boy from a passing school bus. The woman waved, and the whole side of the bus waved back.

This place is pretty friendly after all, I thought. Now all they have to do is paint a smile on that bear at the Black Bear Restaurant.

13

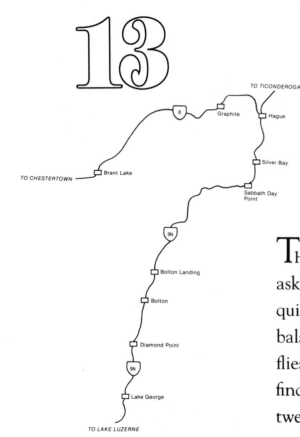

**LAKE GEORGE, DIAMOND POINT, BOLTON,
BOLTON LANDING, SABBATH DAY POINT,
SILVER BAY, HAGUE, GRAPHITE, BRANT LAKE**

THE Adirondacks have long held attraction to those who ask nothing more of the area than to be immersed in its quiet beauty—to make temporary home under pine and balsam, to climb peaks and fish streams, even to swat black flies. Here, within a vastness of woods and lakes, they find reasonable facsimile of wilderness. A forest primeval, twentieth century style.

114

But for thousands of other visitors, the Adirondacks starts and stops at its eastern boundary, on Lake George. Theirs is a tamer, more social holiday...of resorts at water's edge, fine restaurants, gift shops, entertainment day and night—even a place called Magic Forest for those who care not to sample the real woods.

Lake George's wonderland starts the moment one enters the Park with an offering of "Horoscope Readings." Within a year, this enterprise will be gone. Resort businesses can come and go with a change of season. Next door is a gift shop called "Southwest Traders." Everything the civilized vacationer may or may not need can be found along Route 9. By mid-June most shops are open, though the start of the tourist crunch lies a week or two ahead.

This is a day you still have Million Dollar Beach or the miniature golf course to yourself, a day to watch school kids play their games in the field across the street: softball for the boys, soft talk for the girls. It's a day, too, to stroll the grounds at Fort William Henry and relive history, or check the MINNE-HA-HA, Lake George's big passenger boat. There's plenty going on, even before the season starts.

Far and away, the area's biggest attraction is the lake itself, a blue expanse blending to tree-lined hills on either side. Looking northward, one sees but scant evidence of man's handiwork. Here and there a

shoreline clearing or roofline peeks through, but the trappings of tourism are remarkably hidden from view. Lake George appears to have taken man's onslaught in stride.

But beneath its playful surface, not far from the buoy bobbing in the June breeze at Million Dollar Beach, a pervasive aquatic weedform called Eurasian milfoil has taken root. The recent discovery of Lake George's own monster—as some would term it—has sounded an alarm heard all the way to Albany.

According to one study, less than two acres of the lake contain milfoil, notably at Dunham's Bay on the east side and Huddle Bay near Bolton Landing. Weeds are no stranger to the shallow Adirondack lakes. But this is milfoil, an especially tough variety—and this is Lake George, the "Queen of American Lakes," as its village seal proclaims. These days, it seems everyone has ideas how to make the Queen well again.

"The weeds aren't the real problem," said one old-timer at the Village Park. "We'll get 'em one way or another, even if we have to hand-pull them like the APA is saying. But the lake can't take all this development that's going on."

Others in town agree, citing the problems associated with runaway development in recent years along the lake's shore and drainage basin. The Lake George Association, whose motto is "Protecting the lake

116

since 1885," monitors continuing development of the area. Recently, 12 major developments were approved, mostly between Bolton and Lake George Village—an area already highly developed. The debate continues, with virtually every level of state and local government involved. Lake George has many concerned friends.

Meanwhile, another tourist season begins. A horse-drawn carriage thumps along Canada Street, ladies inspect the woven baskets at the Spinning Wheel, and two village employees replace the faucet on the water fountain at the village park.

"Somehow or other, it seems to get broken every year," said one.

"Yeh, but it gives us our job," replied the other, wrapping the fixture in a towel to protect it from the wrench.

"You're treating this faucet like it'll last for ten years."

"Wanta bet?"

Route 9N follows the shoreline north to Diamond Point— passing condos, motels, resorts without end. Frontage along here is said to routinely top $2000 a foot. At Bolton, one of the older settlements on the lake, an estate is being converted into a condo complex. The weathered cabins across the street resist change. Only a satellite dish in the front-yard separates today from the era of motor courts.

In Bolton Landing, a young man leans against the porch of the

library, reading a book—eyeing a girl. Across the park, a woman posts notice on the bulletin board for a craft fair. Flower boxes at the Chamber of Commerce cabin sparkle with marigolds and petunias. Bolton Landing, too, is anxious for summer.

Despite the pressures of tourism, Bolton Landing retains its charm—especially the side streets. They're made for living.

"What ya going to do?" called a boy to his friend on a bike.

"Wanta go to Anna's?"

"See you there in fifteen minutes."

Now both boys quickened their pace down Stewart Avenue and past the Methodist Church. And why not? This is the magic hour between school and supper…a time to let off a little steam and have fun.

Bolton Landing has always been a resort town. Steamboats plied the nearby waters as early as 1817, carrying passengers a distance of four miles in just one hour. The first hotel, The Mohican House, was built here in 1800. The original Sagamore resort on Green Island dates from 1883. Today's Sagamore includes the restored main hotel and surrounding complex of cottages, condos, and related buildings. Summer employment at the resort is said to equal the off-season population of Bolton Landing itself. Right now, Avon representatives are attending a sales meeting here. The Sagamore is packed with smiling bellringers.

118

A few miles north, Route 9N snakes over the Tongue Mountain Range, an area known for rattlesnakes. At the scenic pulloff, two men were building the base for a new information marker.

"What's the plaque going to say?" I asked.

"No idea."

I tried again. "How far to Silver Bay?"

"Don't know."

This conversation was going nowhere.

"Any signs of rattlesnakes?" Now the talker's eyes lit up. It's not every day you can scare a tourist, especially one who keeps asking silly questions.

"There's one under that rock this big," he said, pointing with his trowel to a rock formation across the road, and stretching his arms wide. I ventured across for a cautious peek, but saw nothing.

"Guess he's sleeping."

"Or maybe he's had his fill of tourists," chuckled the talker. Somehow I doubt that information marker will say much about Tongue Mountain's elusive rattlesnakes.

Rattlesnakes once occupied some of the nearby islands, too. Crown Island had been called Hog Island because of the pigs which settlers had put there to keep the rattlesnakes under control. It is said the

French troops, en route to do battle with the British at Fort William Henry, amused themselves by catching the snakes—even cooking and eating them.

In years past, animals frequently inhabited the islands as well—especially deer which crossed on the ice in search of browse, only to become stranded once spring arrived. Hunters relished such easy prey. But according to legend, on one island near Tongue Mountain a hunter missed his mark. Embarrassed at his error, he quickly yelled the military order, "As you were!" Surprised by the sound of a voice, the deer is said to have frozen in its tracks while the hunter reloaded. To this day, the place is called As You Were Island.

Folklore mixes freely with history along Lake George. Sabbath Day Point supposedly was named for the religious services conducted during an encampment on the point by General Amherst's troops. But others had come before Amherst, and there is evidence Sabbath Day Point actually was named before his visit. Grace Memorial Chapel continues the tradition to this day, offering interdenominational services to the summer colony each Sunday during the season.

The Christian Conference Center is located at Silver Bay. But right now, the only conference in sight is a game of "one-on-one" at one end of an outdoor basketball court. Silver Bay is well-named. The sun's reflection off light sand in this shallow bay gives the water added brightness. Too bad more people aren't around to enjoy the near-perfect day—on land or water.

Hague has escaped the excesses of tourism. Sure, the sign at the intersection proclaims Hague is the home of the National Ice Auger Championships. There's also a reminder that a bass tournament and steak roast are coming this weekend. But that's about it. Hague still is a rural community—a place where ducks share the town park with a vanload of kids. A place, too, where the honor system seems to work at the boat launch: "Please deposit $5 in envelope," says the sign, "& put in steel box in booth. Thank you. Town Board."

No sign announces Graphite. Once, extensive graphite mining was carried on here, with the ore concentrates hauled down the hill to Hague for transport by barge to Ticonderoga. Not many people have reason to live in Graphite these days.

Shadows grow long as you arrive at the Horicon Historical Museum. Still there's time to view the rusting farm equiment in the yard, and a weathered sign for the old Pebloe Hotel on a back wall. A "Tourists Paradise," it says.

Brant Lake circles a quiet pond. The town hall, three churches, a school, garage, firehouse and town beach are here. So is Daby's General

Store, where a young man stood near the LARGE EGGS sign. Finally a car appeared.

"Hey Billy...whatya doing," he called.

With the car parked in the middle of the road, the young man and Billy carried on a leisurely conversation. A few minutes later, a teenager jogged along, pushing a lawn mower. At dusk...

*This June day,
Brant Lake's traffic
is underwhelming.*

122

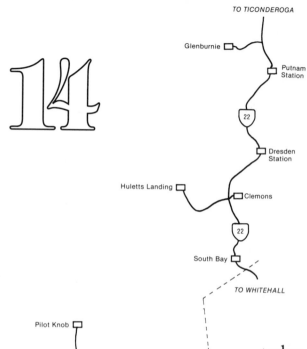

14

ASSEMBLY POINT, KATTSKILL BAY, PILOT KNOB, WEST FORT ANN, SOUTH BAY, CLEMONS, HULETTS LANDING, DRESDEN STATION, GLENBURNIE, PUTNAM STATION

EVERYONE it seems is headed up Route 9L today. And why not? Summer's first day is here...looking just like the airline commercials pictured Florida to be in January. Forget the snow and sleet, the rains and mud. They only make this day sweeter.

Just ask the foursome teeing off at the Queensbury

course, the families opening cottages at Assembly Point and Brayton, the wedding guests at the Harrisina Community Church—or the slightly sunburned boater pulling into Williamson Grocery at Kattskill Bay.

"All winter I keep asking why I stick around here. Then summer comes and I know why."

He pointed to the lake beyond the line of cars, pickups, motorcycles sputtering up the hill.

"It's worth the wait."

A houseboat plows through Kattskill Bay and docked boats wave in its wake. These days practically every square inch of shoreline is dedicated to dock space. Camps are older, closely spaced. Most are occupied this weekend.

Lake George's east side has no through road along its shores to unite one cottage community with the next. The road ends at Pilot Knob where a sign warns the area ahead is PRIVATE. At least the chipmunk that summers behind the sign to Camp Chingachgook greeted me.

The girl in the diner on Route 149 said West Fort Ann stretches all the way to Fort Ann. That made sense. But I found no road sign. Just a sprinkling of houses, a restaurant, a sawmill where turkeys and chickens strut their stuff, and open fields sparkling with the colors of June.

At Aspland's Country Store, a sporty car screeched to a halt

not far from a sleeping dog. As the car pulled away with stereo blaring, the dog uttered a tired bark and rolled over. Even a watchdog deserves a day off now and then.

Route 22 entered the Park at South Bay, north of Whitehall. A few boat trailers are parked at the launch site, and near the shore a farm family picnicked in the shade of a tree. Across the bay, four silos huddled beneath a wooded hill. Northern Washington County is farm country.

What is it that drives some people to the edge with a can of paint—just to tell the world P.K. LOVES L.J? Here, where the road is blasted out of a hillside, there's evidence that TINA & TODD, PAUL AND ELLEN, CRAZY JODY, and SMITTY THE SWIFT also thought such effort worthwhile. Fortunately, the view was nothing special before they arrived.

The turnoff to Clemons wound past an old Baptist Church to the town hall where a rustic wood carving of a pioneer anchors the town flagpole. Neatly posted at the side of the building are the names of those who served their country during World War II. A sign pointed to the Red Top Bar. It was uninhabited except for two tail-wagging dogs.

"Looking for someone special?" The voice came from across the road where a small group gathered around an outdoor grill.

"Not really. I just wanted to see Clemons."

126

"Guess you've pretty much seen it," answered the spokesman. "Most people go over to Lake George."

We talked a bit about fishing, the weed problem on Lake George, what the people do.

"Do you work in town?"

"Over at the fire tower. Put in a lot of hours this time of year."

"Hey gal, cum'on down," called another, sounding like a game show host. A smiling young woman appeared.

"This is the old sawmill," she said. "I've been fixing it into a house."

A walkway stretched along the ridge. Daylilies lined the upper side. Below, a small stream cascaded down the bank, through a hole in the bottom of the dam, to Lake Champlain at the bottom of the hill.

"Used to be a pond," she said. "Going to fix that up, too."

Inside was a kitchen, living area, and a loft accessed by a ladder. In the corner of the living area was an old oak ice chest which she opened. Inside was a stereo player.

"This was my refrigerator 'til last week. But now I've got power."

"You just got electricity?"

"Yep...wired the place myself, too. Worked the first time we plugged in. Lights...music...everything—It's great!"

On my way out I took another look at the woodcarving of the old-timer on the base of the flagpole. Pioneering is alive and well in Clemons, I decided.

Two beaver lodges rise from a large pond on the south side of the road to Huletts Landing. Sure enough, I spotted a furry creature paddling through the lily pads toward a stand of young aspen where stumps outnumbered trees.

The little blue-trimmed post office appears to wear the freshest coat of paint in Huletts Landing. It's alive with flowers, too—border plantings of petunias and marigolds, window boxes of geraniums, hanging baskets...even spires of hollyhock next to the mail drop. Zip 12841 is a tidy place.

But the larger buildings have seen better days. So have the tennis courts and gazebo which overlook the cottages along Lake George's shoreline. Huletts Landing is of another era—an age of hooped skirts, parasols, croquet on the Association lawn. From the top of the hill, the Green Mountains touch clouds beyond the Champlain Valley. Time seems to stand still. So does a doe at the clearing down the hill.

Dresden Station is a short loop off Route 22. The road passes a few houses then dips to the Dresden Inn where someone yells "Hi." Not many cars come this way. Nearby are the tracks of the Delaware and Hudson, but there's no sign of Dresden's station. Lake Champlain peeks through the trees, barely a small stream here.

A boy riding his bike along the narrow road to Glenburnie pulls over while a car passes. He waves to the driver. The golf course and cottages are well-maintained. The man painting a bench at a tee greets the foursome socialslicing an adjacent fairway. Glenburnie has no rough.

Putnam Valley is more like Vermont than the Adirondacks…a gentle land of green pastures, red barns, rolling hills. A sign at a side road pointed the way to food and drink. Now a tractor-drawn wagon showed the way past fields where hay lies freshly cut and swallows dance for their supper. Finally a roadhouse appeared.

"Do you serve food?" I asked the barmaid.

"Maybe we do and maybe we don't. Depends on whether she wants to fix it."

The barmaid pointed to a woman engaged in lively conversation at the other end of the bar. The patrons thought this quite humorous, someone asking for food. I soon got the message and left. On the porch were several straw-lined cages containing an assortment of well-fed pheasants, ducks and geese—obviously not for the table of a hungry traveler. In the distance I could hear a mother call: "Time to eat." I resisted the temptation to answer.

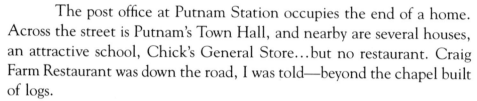

The post office at Putnam Station occupies the end of a home. Across the street is Putnam's Town Hall, and nearby are several houses, an attractive school, Chick's General Store...but no restaurant. Craig Farm Restaurant was down the road, I was told—beyond the chapel built of logs.

As dusk finally settled on the longest day of the year, I arrived at Craig Farm. The building's transformation from barn to restaurant was remarkable...a porch complete with water fountain overlooking fields and woods on the lower level, the main dining area at ground level, and additional dining space in the loft.

The hostess told how she and her husband had come from Philadelphia a few years before to start a cross-country ski center.

"Then we discovered the food was doing better than the skiing. So we converted the barn into a restaurant."

The hostess spoke with justified pride: "This is a special place."

The night was not dark. A full moon pushed clouds across the valley, guiding the weary traveler to Rogers Rock on Lake George. A perfect night for camping.

130

"...a gentle land
of green pastures,
red barns,
rolling hills."

15

**TICONDEROGA
CHILSON
PARADOX
SEVERANCE
NORTH HUDSON
BLUE RIDGE
SCHROON LAKE**

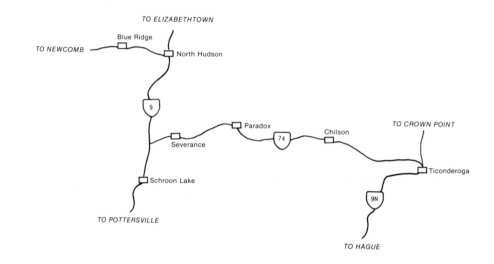

BY 7:30 this Sunday morning, more than coffee is perking at Rogers Rock State Park. The whine of a generator on a motor home had brought much of the campground to life a half hour before. Now a large lady putt-putts her way to the showers on a moped, and Mr. Airstream turns his portable

up a notch to catch the weather report from Schenectady. That got the late-sleepers up.

"How 'bout that!" he exclaimed to a jogger bouncing along with a towel over his shoulder. "It's going up to 75 today!"

The jogger was more impressed with the fish the man was cleaning.

"Did you catch that today?"

"No...last night. It was dark when I got back."

"There's a bass tournament at Hague, you know."

"That's not for me. I get enough competition during the week."

Nearby a father and two sons were pulling stakes, preparing to move on.

"That's Rogers Rock up there," said Dad, pointing to an overhanging formation. As they packed up, he recounted the story of the time Robert Rogers had been pursued by Indians. Finding himself on the edge of the cliff, Rogers escaped by reversing his snowshoes and retracing his tracks from the precipice.

"Hey...neat trick," said one of the boys.

"Is that a true story, Dad?" asked the other.

A few miles up the road, Ticonderoga is starting its day, too. Early Mass is already underway at St. Mary's, a clerk is setting up the outdoor

display at the hardware store, and a few cars are parked in front of the coffee shop. This is a peaceful time to stroll around town...before the Heritage Museum opens and the tourists take over.

The plaque at the museum's entrance tells how Bicentennial Park was created by gifts of land from the Joseph Dixon Crucible Company and International Paper Company. The park occupies the old IP millsite. Federal funding was also involved in the project.

At the covered bridge, a man aims his camera upstream toward LaChute Falls, a scene to be captured a thousand times during the coming months. This pleasant vista may be changing, however, as plans are underway for the development of a hydroelectric plant at the falls.

Still, Ticonderoga has a way of surviving its onslaughts—aesthetic as well as military. Just downstream, what appears to be another covered bridge is actually a support for a wasteline crossing the river. Even the Water Pollution Treatment Facility retains the area's historic integrity. Its design is that of a fort.

Now a car stops at the small park across the street from the treatment plant.

"History's my hobby," said the driver, sounding more like a traveling salesman than historian. Perhaps he worked for the Chamber of Commerce or other tourist organization.

134

"No...I'm from Putnam County. Since I retired, I come here about every weekend."

He paused to read one of the historic markers.

"Can you imagine 18,000 troops coming up the lake? Nothing but boats as far as you can see."

"Must have been some sight."

"Then they climbed Mount Defiance overlooking the fort. You can drive up there, you know."

The tollbooth at the foot of Mount Defiance was in need of repair, and no attendant was on duty. The climb was steep, but short enough—which the old vehicle appreciated almost as much as Burgoyne's troops. According to the history salesman, the mere presence of this armed horde on top of the hill led the disenchanted colonists to give up the fort. Today a flagpole and communications tower share top honors. Below lies the fort, its strategic location all the more evident from this elevation. At the other side of the hill is the village and in the distance, the International Paper mill on Lake Champlain.

Ticonderoga has built its economic base both on industry and tourism. Education, too, for the village houses a branch of North Country Community College in its community building. Not many places in the Adirondacks are as fortunate.

By noon, the parking lot at the fort is nearly filled. This day is hotter than Mr. Airstream had promised, and muggy, too. A redcoat marches across the parking lot to the beat of his drum. Soon the shade of a large maple beckons, and hat, jacket, drum are quickly removed. Enough of history for this young man—at least for a few minutes.

The guide said the fort originally was named Fort Carillon for the musical quality of the LaChute Falls. Built by the French, captured by the British, taken by the colonists, and retaken by the British, the fort's ever-changing stewardship over two wars and twenty years assured its place in history. Early in the 19th century, New York State gave the fort to Columbia University and Union College. Later it was sold to the Pell family, the present owners.

Down at the lake, kids play in the park at the cable crossing, waiting for the ferry's return from the Vermont side. The Fort Ticonderoga Ferry dates its beginning to 1759 when Lord Jeffery Amherst established a crossing service to maintain a supply line between the forts on Lake Champlain and the Connecticut River. Few businesses still operating can claim to be as old. Today, the woman with a hot dog cart near the ferry entrance is doing a brisk business, too.

People who live along Route 74 no doubt could tell you exactly where Chilson starts and ends—from first bump to last. But when you're a stranger in the area, you have to pick more obvious landmarks—like the Hideout Bar, Lark General Store, or the sign to the Putnam Pond Campsite. I imagine these all are in Chilson, along with a few houses, a three-wheeler playing in a field, and two kids playing in a dirt pile.

Paradox was on the map, but apparently not on the road—which is being rebuilt along this stretch. Stone and gravel are piled high here, but Paradox is not to be seen. It is said the lake was so named because its flow often changed direction during spring runoff.

The houses of Severance are neat and closely spaced—as though a pleasant village street had been picked up and moved intact to the country. The post office occupies the wing of one house. Nearby is a garage, TJ's Greenhouse, and a few homes. Severance starts and stops abruptly.

The giant statue of a frontiersman, the likes of which the Adirondacks may never have seen, overlooks the few cars parked at Frontier Town. Their season is yet to start. Inside, at the cafeteria, a woman instructs a college-age boy in the fine points of foodmanship. He doesn't appear too enthused with Cafeteria 101. But that's the price of earning some money for next semester.

Long before its neighboring tourist attraction was conceived, North Hudson was a thriving community. It had a forge, fed by the iron

137

mines at Paradox Lake. Here, too, were charcoal kilns, blacksmith shop, sawmill, ice house, tannery, and a company store.

Some of North Hudson's past survives—notably an old country church perched on a knoll at the edge of the hamlet, and a 19th century Adirondack boarding house which is now a bed and breakfast establishment.

"We've been working on the place constantly since we took it over," said the innkeeper. "Of course, with a place this size and age there's always more to do."

Inside was an attractive dining room with two tables set for guests, and a corner hutch of antiques. Upstairs has a lounge area, two bathrooms with classic bathtubs, and several attractively finished bedrooms. The years may have settled the porch slightly, yet it remains as comfortable as the day it was built. The old boarding house seems to have taken well to its new role.

Across the street is the town hall and a two-vehicle garage used by the fire department. It has an unlisted number, I am told.

"After all, there are only 179 people in the entire town," said the innkeeper. "That's less than one person per square mile."

The few houses and campground of Blue Ridge are incidental to the wild beauty of the area. The Branch River tumbles past to the

Schroon, and the distant mountain ridge indeed has a bluish tint. To the north lies picturesque Elk Lake.

There's talk around Schroon Lake of a new convention center and resort for the town. Plans are still in an early stage, but the prospect of the development clearly has the community excited.

Meanwhile, the daily routine continues. The teepee is up at the entrance to Schroon Lake Campground. Word of Life in South Schroon is expecting 4000 visitors this summer. The Maypine Marina is a beehive of activity, and the town beach is packed with sunbathers. Beyond, a sailboat plays in the breeze as it tacks toward Adirondack.

On Main Street, Schroon Lake's senior class is parading into church for its baccalaureate service. Nearby, a house decorated with crepe paper, balloons, and a CONGRATULATIONS banner awaits the graduates. The woman next door has a front porch view of it all. The future of the village kids was clearly on her mind today.

"If this resort project gets going," she reflects, "maybe…just maybe they won't have to go to Glens Falls or Albany to find a job as soon as they're outa school. Wouldn't that be great?"

No one disagrees on this day of hope. After all, who wants their kids to grow up and leave? Even when a gut feeling keeps saying they might be better off if they did.

16

TO LONG LAKE

Blue Mountain Lake

TO INDIAN LAKE

28

Raquette Lake

28

TO OLD FORGE   Inlet

**INLET
RAQUETTE LAKE
BLUE MOUNTAIN LAKE**

SOME places have the tourist business down to a science. They know how to get travelers to stop and spend some time. Money, too. Inlet seems to have what it takes—a bend in the road to slow you down, a handy place to park the car, even a bench to park the body and watch tourists.

Tourists are easy to spot. Just look for a camera strapped to neck, or a bag strapped to shoulder. You don't see many men loaded down with packages or vacation

140

information. Those things go into the strapped bags women usually carry. Now and then a husband joins his wife in a shop. But most are content to wait in the car, peek in a shop window, or find a spot to sip a cup of coffee.

At the coffee shop, the noon news from Watertown kept fading in and out on Channel 7. Customers alternate sipping with squinting, assuming no doubt the voiceless, squiggly image on screen was the anchor man. Momentarily the sound returned, and the voice of our President came in loud and clear. Finally the picture cleared, too—just in time for a commercial.

"We've got to do something about this TV," said the woman behind the counter. "Reception is terrible."

"Don't you get other stations?" asked the tourist.

"We get Channel 2 in Utica and 3 in Syracuse…but they're both NBC. Sure will be good when we get the cable."

The man at the end of the counter picked up his ears.

"I've given up on TV," he said. "These days I just read. Reading's fundamental, you know."

"So's TV," chuckled the woman, switching to the soap on Channel 2. "Guess I'll just have to miss 'The Young and The Restless' today."

Inlet's summer business is based on more than the passing tourist, of course. People come here from their camps and cottages, the camp-

grounds at Limekiln and Eighth Lakes, and from nearby resorts. A few even come by canoe on their way up the Fulton Chain. Perhaps the town's most notorious guest was Chester Gilette. He, too, enjoyed Inlet's hospitality until his arrest at the Arrowhead Hotel in July, 1905 for the murder of Grace Brown on Big Moose Lake.

Leaving Inlet, a green bus from Adirondack Woodcraft Camp passes, hauling a trailer of canoes. A seaplane gently bobs at the dock of Payne's Air Service, and a few golfers parade the fairway near the turnoff for Limekiln and Moose River Plains. Traffic moves fast today. A car with out-of-state plates flies by, an Adirondack lawn chair roped to its roof. White and yellow daisies sparkle from a roadside clearing. Summer in the woods is short and intense—both on and off the highway.

Most vacationers zip by Raquette Lake with a glance—intent on reaching Saranac, Lake Placid or other destination by day's end. From the road they see but one section of the lake called South Bay, along with a marina, fire house, and a small framed schoolhouse. There's more to Raquette Lake than meets the passing eye.

Fact is, Raquette Lake has nearly 100 miles of shoreline—most of it hidden from Route 28. Here are jagged points and hidden coves, sandy beaches and tree-covered islands. A great place to put a camp and get away from it all. Of course, others have had the same idea. At one time or another during the past 150 years Raquette Lake has been witness to the Adirondack camp in its every form—from the simplest to the most elegant.

The first settlers cleared a few acres of land on the west side of the lake, constructing their crude hunting camps of bark. One of these pioneers, William Wood, was said to have lost the lower half of both legs to frostbite. Still, he was able to continue the rugged life in the wilderness—and at one time even made a trip to Elizabethtown, some 75 miles distance, carrying his own backpack and boat. Clearly, a special breed had chosen to settle here.

Hermit Alvah Dunning also picked Raquette Lake for the site of his camp—first settling on Indian Point and later moving to the camps which the area's first publicist, "Adirondack" Murray, had built on Osprey Island. But times were changing, and the wilderness which provided sanctuary for a hermit also held special attraction for the rich and famous. Their structures, quite naturally, were the ultimate "camps" of Raquette Lake and surrounding area, competing in comfort with the finest summer homes of the Thousand Islands or Newport.

"Camps are still a way of life here," said the captain of the mailboat. "Of course, the places they build now are scaled down from the big old places—the so-called Great Camps."

"There's a vacation house, over there," said the man sitting nearby.

"Maybe that's what you call it. But around here that's a camp."

"A four-letter word to be proud of…huh?"

During the summer months there are enough people in residence around the lake to qualify for mailboat service. But delivering the mail on Raquette can be a challenge, especially on a day the wind kicks up. As the boat approaches a dock, the captain idles down while his young deckhand hands a leather satchel containing the day's mail to outstretched arms on the dock. Wave action and wind conditions add considerably to the excitement of the transfer.

In the distance, a fishing boat cuts the waves around Long Point, headed for the cluster of travel trailers and tents filling the state campsite at Golden Beach. Briefly, the mailboat follows its wake, passing the well maintained buildings of Camp Pine Knot, the first of W. W. Durant's Great Camps in the area. Now it's the Huntington Memorial Outdoor Education Center. Much is different from the days of the Great Camps. Names and stewardship have changed. Massive lodges have given way to simple frame structures or take-along metal homes on wheels. Still, the camp tradition endures.

Raquette Lake hamlet makes no pretenses. It is a summer place,

144

pure and simple. The Raquette Lake Supply Company operates the General Store for the summer people much the same as at the turn of the century when the business was moved from the settlement of Durant on Long Point to its location near the new Raquette Lake Railway Station.

Today, there is no evidence of the station or the adjacent dock for the steamers which plied these waters in the early 1900's. A marina now hugs the north side of the shore above the launch site and town dock where this afternoon a single outboard is docked and another circles to land. Nearby, the white spire of the Raquette Lake Chapel reaches above trees.

Two boys skid their bikes to a halt in front of a hand-lettered banner promoting the upcoming canoe race, fireworks and dance. These days sure are a far cry from winter when nothing's going on and the bus ride from school in Indian Lake is long.

"By the time you get home it's almost dark," said one of the boys. "Just about enough time to run down for a loaf of bread or a quart of milk for Mom—if the store's open, that is."

"But there's good things about winter, too," added his friend. "Like when the old man lets me use the snowmachine and I can go tearing up the road."

"The roads are empty?"

"Not much but snowmachine tracks on the side roads and lake...at least till winter carnival or when they start cutting ice." He pointed to the lake beyond the dock.

"We stay clear of where they cut," smiled his friend.

"The water's kinda cold that time of year."

During the early years of the century, Blue Mountain Lake was two boat rides and a train ride from Raquette Lake. A steamboat would carry passengers across the waters of Raquette and up the Marion River where a train made the seven-eighths mile trip through the Marion River Carry. Travelers then boarded a second lake boat for the journey across Utowana and Eagle Lakes to its destination at Steamboat Landing on Blue Mountain Lake. When the highway came through in the 1920's, the days of the Raquette Lake Transportation Company, which operated the boats and train, were numbered. Steamboats were no match for autos. The trip by road was fast, smooth, uninterrupted—and travel efficiency soon came to be etched in asphalt.

Today cars slow but slightly to pass an elderly biker along the road. How long has it taken him to pedal from Raquette to Blue? About the same amount of time as the lake steamers and train used to take. Now cars make the trip in a few minutes. So what if the journey is a blur? How quickly it is over, how soon we reach destination.

146

Pity the poor biker left behind. He can only watch hawks soar and blue jays squabble. Or squirrels give chase and daisies wave welcome from his roadside garden. Things you see only when you slow down the blur.

Residents of Blue Mountain Lake can thank John Holland for not calling his new inn the Tallow Lake House or Mount Clinch House, for those were the names by which their lake and mountain were then known. Instead, he decided to call his place Blue Mountain Lake House—and the name of the mountain and lake were forever changed. One can only speculate if Tallow Lake or Mount Clinch would have become as famous a resort as Blue Mountain Lake.

Potter's Motor Lodge and Resort now stands near the site of the old Blue Mountain Lake House. To this day, guests from here and Curry's Cottages next door can view the same unspoiled expanse of lake and mountains which first greeted visitors to these shores over a century before. At Steamboat Landing, canoes have replaced steamers for lake transportation. Still, you can retrace the short route of the "Tuscarora" to the Marion River Carry—or embark on a mountain lake and river journey of a hundred miles or more.

The Church of the Transfiguration has stood on the shores of Blue Mountain Lake for over a century. Constructed of logs, this unique house of worship is listed in the National Register of Historic Places. Since many

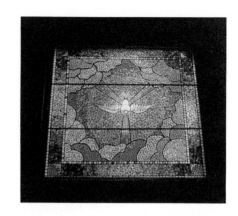

of the early parishioners rowed to church, it faces the lake. Like most of the businesses in the area, the church closes for the cold months.

"Just about everyone who attends service is either a summer resident or visitor," said the church warden. "Only two Episcopal families live here during the winter."

He invited me to take a look at the stained glass windows from inside. Above the altar, deflected sunlight revealed a handsome rendition of a traditional theme—the dove of peace. On the lakeside wall is a contrasting modern treatment of stained glass art depicting the wildlife of the area—flying geese, a paddling duck, a jumping fish, a standing heron, and what appears to be a curious beaver—all against the background of a blue-tinted mountain.

"That's our centennial window," said the warden. "We wanted to honor our wildlife."

Right on cue, a red merganser and two baby ducks paddled by as we left the church. The man was not surprised.

"There are many baby ducks here this year...maybe a dozen," he said. "The adults take turns baby-sitting."

The Adirondack Museum is the Smithsonian of the woods, a depository for its artifacts and illuminator of its history. First-timers to the region should be required to spend a full day here, even if they are not museum buffs. They'd leave with a far better idea of what the Adirondacks are all about.

By early afternoon, the museum's parking lot is nearly filled. Many people have been here before. Some, in fact, make an annual pilgrimage to view the new exhibits and revisit old favorites. The museum includes two dozen buildings in a campus setting atop the hill overlooking Blue Mountain Lake. Designers of the main building thoughtfully placed a picture window at the lake side of the structure to produce what has become for many the museum's favorite exhibit—a spectacular view of Blue Mountain Lake and surrounding mountains.

The Adirondack Lake Center for the Arts offers a remarkable mix of programs. Here you can be trained in the art of making a packbasket or relax to the music of visiting performers. There's something for just about everyone: workshops and craft demonstrations, movie classics, concerts—even a locally-produced annual comedy called "Forever Wild," which seems to have more lives than Rocky, Jaws and Superman combined.

Now a low-flying helicopter roars overhead—headed for the ranger station at Lake Durant with water samples from outlying lakes. In recent years, Adirondack waters have been surveyed, monitored, analyzed like never before. Everyone knows what acid rain does to a mountain

environment. Still, you don't hear much talk about it at the coffee shop, or over at the garage. People here don't talk about pH levels. But they'll tell you fishing's not as good as it used to be.

The chopper now revved up and the yellow-suited attendants moved quickly away from the pad. Moments later the monster was airborne, off for more samples. The loon that summers back in Rock Pond took off, too, but in the opposite direction. Out on the lake...

The fishermen
were not having
much luck today.

150

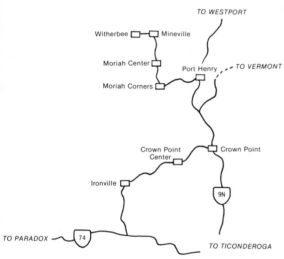

WHEN you turn onto Corduroy Road and head toward Old Furnace Road, automatically you start looking for an historical marker—especially when the road leads to Crown Point, a place oozing with history.

But Corduroy Road must not be on the tourist route. The only sign you see warns BEWARE OF DOG at a house along the way—the one with a friendly dog wagging its tail. Still you continue, bouncing past the cattails and white lilies of Penfield Pond, certain you're headed into the past.

One thing's for sure: Corduroy Road has been here a while. No modern road would rise, dip, bend and twist as much. Today's roadbuilders push hills and blast ledges to make their highways straight—and boring. Corduroy Road still has character. Only its top coat of asphalt is dressed in the 20th century. You wouldn't be surprised to come upon an ore wagon just around the bend…kicking dust, headed for the foundry at old Irondale.

Sure enough, around the bend was Ironville (as Irondale came to be called)—its buildings and church neatly fenced and painted white, flags flying in front of the Penfield Homestead across from a small village green. Only the ore wagon was missing. Even so, the scene was more of the last century than today. And more of New England than the Adirondacks. Not surprising, since Allen Penfield, who settled here to build his forge and trip-hammers, was a native of Vermont.

Today, the entire hamlet is an historic district, with Penfield's home and adjacent outbuildings serving as a museum. Several rooms of the homestead remain furnished much as they were in the 19th century. Others house memorabilia and exhibits of the community's industrial past, including a replica of the electromagnet used in the Penfield iron operations.

"This was the first industrial use of electricity," said our guide.

She explained the original electromagnet had been sold to a Vermonter, Thomas Davenport, in 1833. This blacksmith-turned-inventor used the device for experiments which led ultimately to the development of the electric motor.

Putnam's Creek once powered dozens of mills and production operations on its fast-flowing journey downhill to Lake Champlain. Over 100 waterwheels were said to be along the creek. Today, little evidence remains of this early industry.

"Any of these roads will get you to Crown Point Center," said the lady behind the picket fence. I chose the road most traveled, Middle Road…soon passing a house with a dish antenna in the yard. Now I had returned to real time.

Shortly the roads all converged at a little triangle of green sprinkled with field flowers. Across the street was The McCabe Store which, for the moment at least, appeared to be as empty as the intersection. Is this Crown Point Center? Down the street someone was scraping old paint off a railing at the Methodist Church.

"Yep…this is Crown Point Center," he reported. "Used to have its own post office, but no more."

A post office is important. Once it's gone, a place seems to lose its identity. After a while, those who pass through have no idea where they are. But the young mother who's pushing a stroller knows. So does the old man who greets her from his frontyard garden. Regardless of what the postmarks say, this will always be Crown Point Center—a neighborly place where one can stop to talk for a few minutes and depart with a plump squash in the stroller.

At Crown Point, a pulp truck pulled into the Getty Convenience Store just as the noon whistle blew—its driver deciding to take his lunch break before unloading at the IP plant in Ticonderoga. Two visitors from New Jersey parked their car near the village green to view the Civil War monument and stroll around the gazebo. There, an unfriendly dog on a leash sent them in the direction of the First Congregational Church at the opposite end of the green. Guess the gazebo doubles as a doghouse.

A little later, the mother with toddler-in-hand and squash-in-stroller made it to the grocery store. No doubt she's got it figured out how to get home with the squash and toddler—plus a bag or two of groceries. The stroller is coming in handy.

The road crew is patching a stretch along Route 9N, making the most of a fickle season. Now a dark cloud passes over Fort Crown Point, and an older couple scamper from car to pavilion with picnic basket in tow. Moments later, a soft rain falls on a mother and two girls walking the upper path overlooking the ancient fort.

"It's raining…it's pouring…," sing-songed the younger child. But before she could continue, the rain stopped. Eyeing her father at the bottom of the hill, she flew off in his direction yelling: "Daddy! Daddy! it rained!" Her sister, having no part of the weather bulletin, stayed behind to take another picture of the fort above the strategic narrows of the lake.

History will be reenacted at Crown Point next weekend when participants representing the forces of the Crown clash with Washington's Continental troops in a key battle of the Revolution. But on this day all is peaceful at the fort. Only picnickers invade; only a child's camera takes a shot.

Up the road, Port Henry has been witness to an encounter of another sort—sightings of the Lake Champlain monster. Many communities display an honor roll of sons and daughters who have served their country. But here the roll gives recognition to those who have sighted Champ, as the monster has come to be called. Over 100 sightings are tabulated, the first being Samuel de Champlain himself, in 1609.

People around Port Henry take their monster seriously. In fact, a few years ago the community passed a resolution declaring the lake's waters off limits to any who might "harm, harass or destroy" the apparition. Monsterbusters beware! Of course, should Champ ever turn out to be a Jaws with long tail, that resolution could quickly be voided.

But until proved otherwise, Champ remains a friend of man, and tourist. The Champ passenger bus, which plies the roads along the valley, depicts a benign character on its side. And the Chamber of Commerce float which is anchored along Route 22 between parades, shows a bright-eyed whimsical Champ that wouldn't harm a mosquito. Or lamprey.

Behind the float, several ice shanties are stored in a neat row. Next winter, when the lake is frozen, they will be moved onto the ice together with hundreds of other shanties. Imagine the fish stories generated by a community of fishermen! There might even be another sighting of Champ.

Things have changed around Port Henry. Gone are the nearby mines which for years provided the area's economic base. Gone, too, are many of the old landmarks. But others are finding new life as downtown is being revitalized. The Lee House has been made into apartments, the railroad station houses Moriah's Senior Center, and the old Essex Theater has become Jimmy's Newsroom.

Downtown shoppers pass a small park created from a former building site. A salesman enjoys a quiet lunch on the green at the town hall occupying a large brick Victorian structure. Flowers bloom from a circular planter in the street. Civic pride is everywhere. You sense the enthusiasm. Port Henry's residents should drive around with a bumper sticker proclaiming "I'M THE REAL CHAMP!"

Moriah Corners is off the main road just far enough to be on its own. It's a place a boy can teach his kid brother to ride a two-wheeler without worrying about traffic. A place, too, where a fresh coat of paint on a house might raise a comment, and a new color raise an eyebrow. Change comes slowly here. Even the church retains its old sign MORIAH BAPTIST CHURCH 1828 along with a second sign for the MORIAH METHODIST COMMUNITY CENTER. Whatever its present denomination, the church looks comfortable. So does the general store at the corner, and the restored older homes around the corner where a woman is perched on a ladder painting the trim on her front porch. But she's not changing colors.

Further along, the roads intersect at what must be Moriah Center, though no sign is here. Just a gas station, ambulance center, a few houses, and another general store where the soft drink truck from Glens Falls has stopped to make a delivery. On cue, the girls standing in front giggle as the young man pushed a beverage cart through the door. Suddenly the wind picked up and the CAR FOR SALE AS IS sign broke loose from the store bulletin board. The girls chased after it, still giggling. "Lookit that #-$-%-*-! wind," exclaimed the man leaving the store. Despite what the song says, not everyone calls the wind Moriah…in Moriah.

At Mineville, a busload of children from the summer recreation program pulled in at the corner. Excited voices awoke the dog stretched across the sidewalk, but only briefly. Soon it was asleep again on the grass strip a few feet away.

At first, Witherbee appeared abandoned. To be sure, a few cars were parked along the street but no one was in sight. As soon as I stopped, however, four kids bounced from a row house.

"It's OK to take pictures of the mine," said a girl, pointing in the direction of an abandoned building across the street. "People do it all the time." I had the feeling not many had been around lately.

Camera in hand, I left the kids playing under a line of wash and walked behind Republic Steel's old building. Not much of a picture here. Just a deep excavation and a slag pile on the opposite side. There's been talk in recent years the tailings might be recycled to recover apatite, from which a variety of rare earth minerals used in microelectronics can be extracted. But for now the pile is untouched.

When I returned the children had disappeared. Witherbee again was deserted. Now the wash waved wildly in the quickening breeze and storm clouds darkened skies behind the church with a bent cross but no name. Witherbee has weathered storms before. Still you wonder if these kids will be here when they grow up, working the tailings for a mineral they never heard of—and hanging wash for their children?

18

**WESTPORT, WADHAMS,
WHALLONSBURG, BOQUET,
ESSEX, WILLSBORO,
KEESEVILLE, PORT DOUGLAS,
PORT KENT, AUSABLE CHASM, VALCOUR**

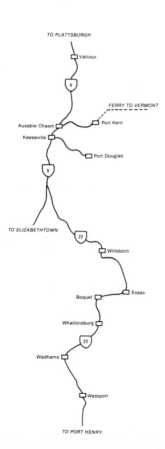

At first glance, Amtrak's little passenger station in Westport might be mistaken for a crate of glass and steel that's been dropped alongside the elegant old station—ready for loading onto the next train out of town.

But things are not always as they appear in Westport. The turn-of-the-century station has become the Depot Theater and Art Center. And what looks to be a crate is

160

indeed the passenger station—at least for now. Yet you sense the little station's days are numbered. Steel and glass don't mix with gingerbread.

With few exceptions, Westport has managed to keep the 20th century at arm's length. Why not see for yourself? Step beyond the shops on Main Street, past The Inn on the Library Lawn. Here's where hollyhocks bask in the morning sun and wraparound verandas bid welcome to an era of porch swings and wicker furniture—a time of easy living, simple pleasures. What you see is no replica of the past. Westport is for real.

Its streets are seldom overrun with tourists. After all, a stroll through yesterday is not for everyone. But that's okay with the old-timer shuffling down the sidewalk; his favorite bench is empty and waiting. The kids running around the park are happy, too. They've got the lawn to themselves while Mom waits for the library to open.

A game of tag is about as exciting as it gets—except on the Fourth of July. That's when the town celebrates with everything from a parade to fireworks…games for the kids, tug-of-war for the sturdy, chicken barbecue for the hungry, a "heritage" dance for the light-footed. There's even the Westport "500." It's enough excitement to last the year!

And it does. Next day you're back at your shady spot with a book…daydreaming while boats bob in the bay, and Westport again

161

weaves its magic. Only a pulp truck chugging through town awakes you to the world beyond Gingerbread Street.

The one-room schoolhouse south of the village held Westport's children for a hundred years. Built early in the 19th century, this little limestone structure appears fit for another century. For now school's out, and swallows chase the insects of summer above the ancient yard.

Down the road, Camp Dudley, too, is quiet—the lawns and playing fields empty. But Camp Dudley is still in business. After all, the historic marker in front reports it's "the oldest boys camp in continuous operation in the United States."

Early in the nineteenth century, General Luman Wadhams selected a site for his sawmill and gristmill along the fast-flowing Boquet River. A forge also was established at the same time as Wadhams' mills. Soon a furniture shop, blacksmith shop and other businesses were added. By mid-century, Wadhams could boast a population of 1300. Now, the early businesses are gone and the population has shrunk to 200. However, one plant still stands along the Boquet's rocky shore.

"That's our power plant," said the man on the bridge with obvious pride. "The oldest one still going in the state." "Actually, it's the second oldest," corrected the young man unloading lumber at the entrance. "Niagara Mohawk has one a little older down in the Albany area."

162

"What's the crane doing in the riverbed?" I asked.

"We're putting in another generator. That'll give us 150 kw more output in the spring…and backup for the rest of the year, too."

The old plant looked quite like a museum, except the turbine and belt-driven generator were still huffing and puffing through their chores. Today, the 150-kw generator was on-line, with the 300-kw unit as backup. Old panel-mounted meters on the control board monitored output, and the original knife switches were in use. Still, years of idleness had taken its toll.

"Sure was a job to get everything going again," said the young man. "Had to rebuild the turbines and generators…and replace the penstock. Even the dam had to be rebuilt."

Originally, the electricity produced was intended to power a high temperature furnace for glassblowing. But plans changed.

"Some day we might get back to glassblowing," he said, pointing to some lightly tinted glassware gathering dust at a window. For now, the attractive pieces appeared quite at home in the filtered sunlight of a turn-of-the century hydroelectric plant.

How come some country people allow old machines and debris to pile up in their yard? Will a discarded washing machine ever be repaired, a scrapped car returned to use? Probably not. Maybe they'll be used for spare

parts, or someone will come along and want something on the pile? Junkpiles never seem to shrink. This rural dwelling continues to live with its past—right in the sideyard. And just down the road is a community gushing with civility. Guess it's all a part of the Adirondack mix.

Here and there along the road the remains of an early farm-house or barn can be seen…a cellar hole covered with brush…a falling silo…overgrown fields and broken fences… memories of the small family farms which once claimed this valley. Now, clusters of trim buildings and silos rise from lush fields of grain and corn, holsteins graze hillside meadows, machines take the hard work out of cutting, thrashing, baling, and other labors of the land. After 200 years, this narrow strip between lake and mountain still serves its tenants.

In the distance, you spot a church spire rising from a field. Soon the roofs of a half dozen houses appear. Sure enough this is Whallonsburg, where the volunteer fire department sponsors bingo on Thursdays at the P of H 194 Grange Hall, and the garage still displays a sign of the flying red horse.

There are other signs of the past, too. The old house next to the Methodist Church is being restored—new doors installed, the inside gutted and rebuilt. The former schoolhouse is getting a fresh coat of yellow paint. But Whallonsburg is hardly the community it once was.

164

Gone are the shirt factory, wheelwright, sash and blind factory, sawmill, forge, and hotel. These days, if a salesman happens along it's only to take the scenic route to the larger lakeside communities. The Northway is the route of commerce. Whallonsburg is for those who wish to cast for trout and salmon, or glimpse the pastoral valley life.

Gradually Boquet's mountains close on pasture and meadow. A truck from the Weatherization Program is parked near a trailer while workers insulate and enclose its underside. Next winter's winds will be less noticed here.

Once Boquet had a woolen mill, and sheep grazed these hills. The place also had a nail factory and forge. Now Boquet is a bend in the road where a gentle breeze stirs the wash hanging next to the octagonal schoolhouse. Built in 1826, it is listed in the National Register of Historic Places. Boquet has another historic building—the Chapel of the Nazarene which was built before the Civil War. This house of worship has no spire, yet architecturally reaches skyward with vertical board and battens, narrow elongated windows, and a steep dual-pitched roof—all in perfect symmetry.

Briefly, Lake Champlain and the hills of Vermont loom in the distance. Then the road abruptly drops into the picturesque lakeside community of Essex. Here, along shade-lined streets are outstanding

165

examples of Greek Revival, Federal, and Victorian architecture. The entire hamlet has been designated a National Historic District.

Essex has no shortage of craft and antique shops, either. You'll find hand-carved birds, fashions of a past era, period furniture, new copies of LIFE magazine from the 40's. At Sugar Hill Pottery, you can watch the creation of a bowl. And just a few doors away, you can watch the restoration of a home. That's Essex's best-known craft.

The porch of the Essex Inn crowds the sidewalk only because it was there first. But look at the front-row seat it offers. See the lady examining a chair at the antique shop? The two men rebuilding the front entrance across the street? The girl patting the black dog in front of the post office? Bet you can follow the dog's every step from the rocking chair. Sure enough, here's a wag…there's a sniff. Up one side it goes to the town offices…then down the other side to where the potter's dog naps at Sugar Hill. Nothing clutters your view from here. You know Essex is an easygoing, comfortable place, especially between ferries on a warm summer afternoon.

A lot of water has gone over Willsboro's dam since William Gilliland first built it in 1765. Sawmills, pulpmill, and other industries have come and gone. Just below the dam, an old gristmill still stands. The blue limestone used in its walls is said to have come from the same quarry on Willsboro Point which produced stone for the Brooklyn Bridge and New York's Capitol in Albany.

These days the dam on the Boquet is witness to a different activity, the spawning run of salmon. A baffled fishway allows fish to bypass the eight-foot dam while restricting the upstream movement of lampreys, a destructive vertebrate. Before being released from a holding tank, the salmon are examined, and eggs collected. Today the fishway is not operating. But that will change in a few weeks when the spawning run starts.

Right now, a state trooper's car is making a run across the bridge, siren blaring. Moments later the car with flashing lights pulled up at a house with lights of its own—the decoration of a Christmas past. Two boys passing on bikes pulled off to watch. Can't miss excitement like this. But there was none. Soon the trooper drove off, lights out, siren stilled. Again, all is peaceful along the Boquet.

"Is this the road to Port Douglas?" I asked the young girls at the information booth.

"Isn't Port Douglas a suburb of Keeseville?" questioned one of the girls.

"I think I went swimming there once," said the other.

Perhaps Keeseville should be the next stop, I thought, turning on the radio. The French-language station came in better than Schenectady. That seemed right. After all, the Dutch got as far as Schenectady—but not up here. This was French territory. So I settled back to soft music...and the melodic language which white man first spoke along Champlain's valley.

Keeseville's Industrial Park is ready for business when and if it comes to this corner of the Adirondacks. For now, its divided entrance soon leads to woods—a trail paved with hope for the future. Meanwhile, Route 9 handles Keeseville's commerce.

Downtown has the stores and services you'd expect including the Village 5&10 and Pearl's Department Store. The Stewart's shop on the corner supports the cause of local education by promoting a tie-in with the Summer Reading Club at Keeseville Free Library. "Read, Report and Earn Free Stewart's Cones and Sundaes" promises a sign on the wall.

Across the street, colorful butterfly cutouts are displayed in the window of the Cubby Hole Gift Shop. But the Cubby Hole has more than gifts. It's the headquarters of Murphy's Cabs, which Mrs. Murphy operates from a desk in the corner. These days she wears the only cabby's cap in town.

On the tennis courts up the hill, two boys are playing their own version of the sport. "Over-the-fence" it might be called, for that's where the balls went with each wanton swing. The building nearby appears to have been a church in its earlier days. Perhaps it later had been a store, judging from a faded Benjamin Moore sign above the entrance. A community's history often is etched on the face of its buildings. Today, children sit on its steps, giggling at the antics of the "tennis" players.

"How do I get to Port Douglas?" I asked the man leaving NAPA Auto Parts.

"Let's see...go to the corner. Wait...you're parked here. So go the other way to the next corner and take a left. No...take a right, then a left. It's straight ahead 'til you get to the barn and some other things. Maybe three miles...no...not that far."

Port Douglas, it turned out, was easier found than charted. The lakeside settlement overlooked a tugboat and its brood of bobbing pleasure craft. Today the wind blows strong, and the beach is empty except for gulls. This is not a big day in Port Douglas.

Port Kent has more activity. A line of cars awaits the arrival of the ferry from Vermont. Some people do their waiting at the Northern Expressions Gift Shop or the restaurant. A few walk the stretch of beach. Finally, the ferry toots its arrival and the travelers scamper back to their cars. A group of bikers are the first off. The hill ahead is steep, and at the top they pause. "Is this the Adirondacks?" asked one. On cue, two deer

emerged from the woods across the fairway—answering the biker's question better than an entrance sign.

Ausable Chasm is called the oldest tourist attraction in New York State. It has been in operation since 1870. People here are expert at moving traffic from the road to the restaurant and entrance to the boat ride. The view from the bridge over the river on Route 9 gives an excellent idea of the scenic wonder below. A few houses line a side street. But Ausable Chasm's Main Street is the chasm itself.

Valcour is a strip of restaurants, motels, marinas intermixed with homes at the northeastern edge of the Park. The Plattsburgh Air Force Base lies just beyond the boundary, yet close enough for a low-flying bomber to startle unsuspecting visitors.

"You get used to it after a while," said the waitress. Still, some guests at Valcour's motels don't realize how close they are to a SAC base.

"When the bombers come in with their landing lights on, people sometimes run out in their pajamas. Guess they think it's a UFO."

At dusk, quiet claims the shoreline. Ripples replace waves, the lights of a city across the lake squint from distant hills, and a faint moon previews the night above Ausable Point. Now is the time for young people to gather at the beach…for campfires to burn…for cricket and frog to sing the joy of a summer eve.

"…a faint moon previews the night above Ausable Point."

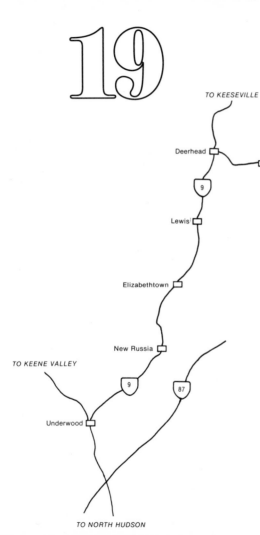

TO KEESEVILLE

Deerhead

Reber

9

Lewis

Elizabethtown

New Russia

TO KEENE VALLEY

9

87

Underwood

TO NORTH HUDSON

**UNDERWOOD, NEW RUSSIA,
ELIZABETHTOWN,
LEWIS, REBER,
DEERHEAD**

THE Northway is not your typical ho-hum turnpike—certainly not that section cutting through the eastern Adirondacks. PARADE magazine once called the 23-mile stretch between Lake George and Pottersville the most scenic highway in the country.

Few who drive the road this August day would dispute that claim. The campers trailing Holiday Ramblers and Apaches know the roads to wilderness don't come any

172

smoother than this. The vacationers on their way to Montreal or New York won't find a prettier view than here. Even the car hauler who's traveled the road a hundred times pauses with his load of sparkling Chevys to glimpse the ancient hills.

Amid such grandeur, Underwood barely rates a glance from Exit 30. This is a place you go through, not to—unless you belong to the Underwood Club. MEMBERS ONLY says the sign in front of a house. Across the street are several cottages, a tennis court and swing set. For the moment, no one is around. How come a place like this makes the map? Maybe there was more to Underwood in years past.

That was the case with Euba Mills up the road. Once it was a thriving settlement. But shortly after the turn of the century, the place was consumed by forest fire and never rebuilt. Chances are, Euba Mills' days were numbered even without a fire.

Not everything has changed around here. The young Boquet River still takes a nose dive at Split Rock Falls where plunging water once powered a trip-hammer and trompe forge. Downstream, the river is more cobblestones than water today. But a hard rain can change the Boquet's personality in a hurry. The people living here know its moods. They know the swimming holes and where to cast for trout or salmon.

Route 9 is yesterday's tourist route. A small motel along the road has a FOR SALE sign. Nearby, turkeys parade through an unfenced yard, and Rhode Island Reds flutter from the path of an approaching truck. A few moments later they're back on the shoulder, again pecking at the gravel.

New Russia doesn't miss the traffic. So what if the Northway has taken most of the tourists? Or if the Greyhound rolls through without stopping—like the place doesn't exist? Who cares? The St. Regis String Band still comes to the social center. The mail still comes to the post office. And people can still do their own thing. If they want to haul the living room rug out to air in the frontyard, that's OK. If they turn up their dual-speaker hamlet blaster before you get to the corner, that's OK, too. Nothing's within earshot anyway, except the mourning doves on the utility pole. And they'll just whir-r-r-r off to another perch—beyond the radio vibes from Plattsburgh, beyond the hum of the sawmill.

New Russia's name dates from the days when czarist Russia was known for its high quality iron. With an eye to marketing their own iron, someone suggested the name New Russia for their settlement along the Boquet. After all, the forge starting up at the falls also produced a high quality iron. So New Russia it became, and New Russia it remains long after its iron age has passed.

The surrounding farmland had a more pastoral beginning. Those

who settled from Vermont called the area Pleasant Valley, for indeed it was. Despite a short growing season, corn still grows high, and kitchen gardens thrive. It takes but a few acres and a few cows to make a good life in Pleasant Valley.

Elizabethtown is in full swing by midmorning. The old-timers who golf daily at Cobble Hill already are walking off the 9th green. A group of kids in green tee-shirts of the summer rec program march past the Deerhead Inn—tennis rackets and ball gloves in hand. Nearby, a teenager loaded with suitcases anxiously awaits the arrival of her ride to summer camp. At the Court House across the street a few people come and go. Once many years before, people gathered here to pay homage to abolitionist John Brown, whose body lay in state on its way to Brown's farm in North Elba.

The town offices are just up the street from the county buildings. Elizabethtown once had village offices, too, until residents voted to abolish this third level of government. Even so, Elizabethtown is not lacking for officialdom. County buildings of one type or another are scattered about the community, including the Adirondack Center Museum where workers this day raised scaffolding in preparation for pargeting and exterior repairs.

"This used to be the high school," said one of the museum

volunteers. "It's also headquarters for the Essex County Historical Society."

"You know, Essex County is the most interesting county in the state," added another volunteer with a smile as broad as her sun hat. "We've a lot going on these days."

Among other things, the museum has compiled a source book of county history and is working closely with schools to further utilize the museum's displays and exhibits—including a sound and light dramatization of the early military struggle for control of the strategic Champlain waterway.

Another of the museum's displays combines the artifacts of a pioneer home in the county with excerpts from the diary of the wife of Adolphus Sheldon, who settled in Ticonderoga shortly after the Revolution. Mrs. Sheldon described her life in the wilderness:

"When I had nothing to do I helped my husband. I did not care what I wore, had, or did, anything to help him. We lived, as you might say on work and love."

At the Colonial Garden behind the museum, a mother and child relax in the summer house. The handsome formal garden abounds in yellows and purples this time of year. On the lawn in front of the garden, county workers were erecting a large tent.

"What's the occasion?" I asked one of them, expecting some historical event was about to unfold.

"Haven't the slightest idea. They don't tell us anything."

"I've got an idea," chimed in another. "Let's get a keg and have a party." The others chuckled at the thought. But the Mountain Valley In-Home Services across the street had different plans. "Tomorrow," the receptionist told me, "we're using the tent for our Aides Recognition Day." Looks like the crew will have to find another place for their party.

The Hand House is a part of the Historic District on River Street. This outstanding example of Greek Revival, built in 1849 by Augustus C. Hand, depicts yet another dimension of early Adirondack life.

The rest of Elizabethtown can be viewed in a minute or two—a few shops and restaurants, the small frame house serving as headquarters for the Adirondack Council, the Town Clerk's home and office ringed with flowers…and the usual assortment of village dwellings including one with a sign for night crawlers and smelt bait. Take away the county activities, and Elizabethtown is another mountain hamlet.

The school bus had just dropped off the kids in Lewis from the summer rec program.

"Did you beat 'em?" asked one of the teenagers sitting on the porch at Parker's General Store.

"Naw…didn't even play 'em," replied the boy with the glove.

Across the street, a woman paused at the First Congretational Church with her two grandchildren.

"That church was here when I came…and it's here when I'm leaving," she said. The children and their parents had arrived from out-of-state the day before. "I just want to show them around one last time. After all, I've been here nearly fifty years."

"Watch…I can pop flowers," said the little boy, pushing a small bloom against his wrist. The significance of their walk escaped him.

"That's something his father used to do when he was a kid," said the woman. "He taught him how to do it last night."

You know they'll all miss Lewis.

But as one chapter ends, another starts. A young couple recently moved their small manufacturing business to town. Today, four sewing machines are humming away, making Softbags.

"It's a great spot to work," said the young man. "And you sure can't beat the view," added his wife.

The Meadowmount School for Strings is on Discovery Mountain, a short distance east of Lewis. During the summer, talented young musicians gather here to study at the former estate of John Milholland, inventor of the pneumatic tube. This afternoon, a group of young people

178

relax on the hill high above rolling fields. Meadowmount is well named.

"Is this Reber?" I asked the boys who were moving baled hay from truck to barn on the corner. They were amused. Not often a stranger comes here asking questions—especially one with a camera around his neck.

"You can drive this way for a couple of farms, and that's Reber," said one of the boys, pointing down the road. "Or you can drive that way." He pointed in the other direction. "At least as far as the church—and maybe further."

"You just can't get Reber in one picture," said another. They all laughed. I was in no hurry to leave the fresh conversation, or the smell of fresh hay.

Sure enough, just over the hill, the steeple of the Reber Methodist Church came into view. The church has been here since 1875. The bridge crosses the North Branch of the Boquet, barely a meadowland stream this time of year. Once a sawmill, forge, and carding mill were here.

The mills may be long gone but Reber Valley is still farm country...a place where cows swish away the flies and white moths flutter away the day...a land of rolling pastures and hillside meadows between mountain and lake.

Ghost cabins claim a stretch of roadside at Deerhead. Back in the 30's, those lucky enough to have frontage on Route 9 often got into the thriving motor court business. Then cabins sparkled with fresh paint and flower boxes—often with porches barely large enough for a rocker. But that's all it took to sit out and talk with your next-door neighbor on his little porch about how your Model A was doing and where you were headed next day. These places were cute, and so were their names—like Donner and Blitzen and the other reindeer. Of course, the names of the Dionne quintuplets were a favorite if you had five cabins.

Now paint has faded and porches dip. But unlike the Burma Shave signs, not all overnight cabins have disappeared. A few actually have found new life. SECONDHAND ANTIQUES says the sign in front of one motor court, with no fear of redundancy. Somehow you hoped Marie, Annette, Emily, Cecile, and Yvonne would do better.

DWYER CORNERS, KEESE CORNERS, HARKNESS, FERRONA, CLINTONVILLE, AUSABLE FORKS, BLACK BROOK, SWASTIKA, WILMINGTON, JAY, UPPER JAY, KEENE, KEENE VALLEY, ST. HUBERTS

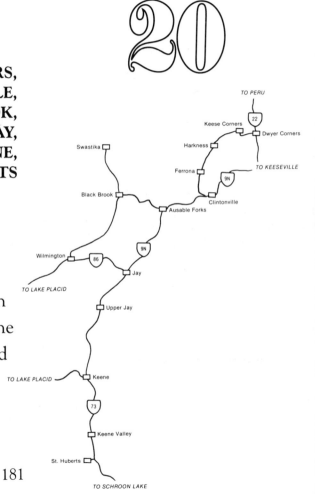

B Y 7:30 in the morning, a steady stream of cars moves through Dwyer Corners as commuters head for work. But traffic at the northeast edge of the Adirondacks is mostly in one direction. Out of the Park. It's much the same along the Park's other boundaries—a daily exodus to shop, factory and office a safe distance from wooded hills and quiet waters. Living in the Adirondacks can be great—providing you don't need a job just down the street.

Houses claim three of Dwyer Corners. The settlement appears to be little else—unless you include the lush apple orchards lining Route 22, or the neatly staked rows of a new orchard along the intersecting road. Payday is a long way off for that field. Beyond, the early sun catches roofs and silo of a dairy farm.

Richard Keese left his mark on the Adirondacks. Keeseville is named for him. So is Keese Corners, where the family homestead has the corner to itself. Not much has changed here over the years. According to the historical marker, the seventh lineal descendant of Richard Keese now occupies this elegant country home with the towering maples and impressive entrance.

Harkness doesn't have many visitors. Maybe that's why people wave as you drive through even when they don't know you. It seems the friendly thing to do. But stop to take a picture of the Methodist Church, or one of the other sights in town. Then you're greeted with silence, and a stare that says, "What are you doing here anyway?" A fine line separates visitor from invader in small towns.

Someone said there used to be a nail factory at Ferrona. Today only brush and scrub trees are in evidence. No clue of a Ferrona, past or present.

Clintonville was a boom town when the iron mines were operating—one of the bright spots in this corner of the Adirondacks. Not much shines in Clintonville these days. A few older houses survive, along with St. Catherine's Catholic Church, the offices for the Ausable Valley Central School, a picnic area tucked between road and river…and a store selling Michigans.

"What's a Michigan?" I asked.

"It's a hot dog covered with meat sauce in a steam roll. Would you like one?"

"Just curious about the name. Never heard of it."

"They're popular up this way. One place in Plattsburgh sells them almost exclusively." The man was an expert. "But ask for a Michigan downstate and they'd probably send you to Detroit."

"That's just what I want," said the man coming in. "Two Detroits…and a six-pack of Miller's." Wonder if there's a ball game around Clintonville this morning?

Traffic had backed up across the bridge at Ausable Forks. Must be a busy place. But soon you discover the bridge is being repaired and one lane is closed. So is the movie theater, the clothing store, and several other places along the street.

Ausable Forks wasn't always this way. For years it thrived—a center of industry and commerce. What better place to establish a mill

183

than where the Ausable's East and West Branches meet? By the early nineteenth century sawmills already were operating here, and with the discovery of iron on nearby Palmer Hill a four-fire forge was soon added. Later came the railroad and the papermill. The community which developed around these industries reflected the area's good fortune.

Now things have changed. Ausable Forks is a milltown without a mill. Many places in the Adirondacks never had an industry—or shops along Main Street which had to close when the community's economic base eroded. Perhaps they're better off.

"I guess you might call us a residential town," said the man standing in front of an empty store. "Now people drive to Plattsburgh or Champlain or Malone for work. Some work as prison guards."

"Guess they still like to live here."

"It's our town. Let me show you what it used to be."

Inside, from a pile of papers on the desk he uncovered an old photograph of the stagecoaches meeting the train.

"Every day the stages would line up at our station waiting for the train to pull in. Then they'd take off with the vacationers—to Paul Smiths, Lake Placid, the Saranacs. All around." Now it's the townspeople who take off.

Gordon's Deli is located in what was Ausable Forks' station house.

Originally this building was a warehouse for the station shown in the old photograph. Later it became the railroad station. Now menus have replaced timetables, but the original woodwork and fixtures are intact, again sparkling. Like the town it serves, the recycled station endures.

The highway crew is patching the road to Black Brook. But there's no delay here, even with one lane closed. Most summer people take the road to Jay.

Not much disturbs the morning peace in Black Brook except the little terrier that yelps at strangers…and its owner who barks "Cum'on, Reject" from across the street. Of course, there aren't many strangers. So there isn't much noise, other than the whining of a power saw behind St. Matthew's.

Too bad Black Brook doesn't have a place where you can sit around and talk. Gauthier's Grocery is too small for that. Almost too small for groceries. But you can still share your porch and views with a neighbor. Maybe catch the breeze blowing over from Taylor Pond, and check on traffic along the old turnpike. That's about the same as people have been doing here for the past hundred years.

My map said I was in Swatstika though the sign along the road calls it Swastika. Guess the people who live here know their own name. Swastika has two houses, one very large woodpile, one falling-down

barn, the ruins of a gas pump—and a growling German police dog to protect the pretty view.

Not many travelers come to Black Brook twice in a season, let alone twice in a day. I had no choice. It's on the only road between Swastika and Wilmington. Black Brook's terrier and owner weren't barking, but the saw was still humming.

Soon woods give way to fields and pastures. Small farms appear. A tractor and hay wagon cling to the edge of Haselton Road as they move from meadow to barn. All is peaceful. But just around the bend is tourist country.

A steady stream of cars arrive and depart the Tourist Information Center in Wilmington.

"Frank, you come here," called a woman from the entrance.

"You're the driver. You listen to the directions."

"See all the stuff I got!" exclaimed a boy carrying out an armful of folders.

"I don't want this scattered all over the car," warned Mother.

"Can I get an ice cream cone at Santa's Workshop?" asked the little boy at their side.

"Cum'on....let's get going," said Father. "The parking lot's going to be packed by the time we get there."

186

It's summer as usual in Wilmington.

Wilmington's Town Park was an oasis. Only a handful of people were on the beach, including a French-speaking family, three boys who had biked over, and two girls who had paddled over. The picnic area was empty—even at high noon. Guess most tourists don't know about the park.

But they sure know about Santa's Workshop. As father had predicted, the parking lot was packed. North Pole has everything you'd expect, including its own post office and zip (12946). Yet somehow the huge MERRY CHRISTMAS above the exit arch fails to bring visions of sugarplums on a hot summer day.

Traffic labors up the steep grade of Whiteface Mountain Memorial Highway. These travelers do their mountain climbing the easy way—even taking an elevator the final 500 feet. Two bikers fly by on their way downhill, shouting "Ho! Ho! Ho!" as they pass Santaland.

Whiteface's Ski Area is popular even in summer. After all, this is the Olympic Mountain, site of the alpine events during the 1980 winter games. Today it matters not that Whiteface has a snow base of zero inches. You can still take a sightseeing ride on the chair lift, walk the hill or picnic under the sign SKI SCHOOL MEETING PLACE.

Vehicles of virtually every description ply the road between Lake

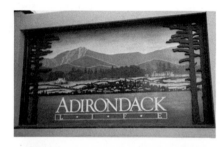

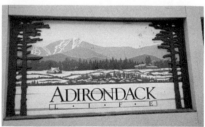

Placid and Wilmington…campers, trailers, cars, pickups, motorcycles, motor homes, bicycles—even motor scooters. If it has wheels, you'll see it. For thousands of vacationers this region is what the Adirondacks are all about. Theirs is not a labored journey to wilderness. Cascading waters are theirs to enjoy, the mountain theirs to conquer from the comfort of car and chair lift.

One might expect vacationers would flock to a place with a village green and a covered bridge—especially when it's only a few miles from Whiteface and Santa's Workshop. But Jay is not for everyone. Its attraction is the quiet life. Too many visitors would be self-defeating:

The boys sitting on the steps of McDonald's General Store which is also the post office—might have other ideas what Jay should be. Maybe they'd like a little more of Lake Placid's excitement. More to do. Like a circus coming to the green this weekend, and not just a craft fair.

It seems you wait all year for summer. When it finally comes, nothing's really changed. Like the the sign ADIRONDACK LIFE put up next to its office in the old church. A summer scene on one side, and the same scene in winter on the other side. Both are pretty…but not much different.

So the boys of Jay sit on the steps of their McDonald's, wishing it were the other McDonald's…watching the Hi-Peaks Kiwanians set up the

188

Coke trailer for their craft fair…waiting for the next stranger to come by and say: "It's just like New England." Especially that pretty girl headed over from THE STORE THAT HAS MOST EVERYTHING, as the sign at Hurley and Madden reads.

"It's the girl that has most everything," jokes one of the boys.

The others laugh loudly, knowing this has to be the highlight of their day. Knowing, too, Jay's not about to change. Really change. It's always going to be a town where you can get your mail and a loaf of bread in the same place.

Across the green, a rummage sale is in full swing.

"You should have been here yesterday," said the lady at the cash box. "We had much more then."

"Is this a church sale?" asked the woman sorting through a table of knickknacks.

"Just three families…but we've got fifteen kids. Amazing what you find when you clean out."

Suddenly the sky darkened as a rain cloud zeroed in on Jay.

"Grab the magazines!" called one of the women.

"Where's that sheet of plastic? I'll get the dresses."

Sprinkle. Shower. Sprinkle. Sun. So goes a mountain rain on a hot afternoon. One cloudful and it's past. But cars crossing the covered

bridge still wear headlights. The dark sky lingers in the surrounding hills.

The kids swimming in the East Branch above the bridge hardly stopped for the rain. Soon they were running around the rocks, laughing and screeching the sounds kids make around water. Again, their mothers relaxed in lawn chairs on the big flat rock in the middle of the river, watching and talking. Who needs a beach when you've got a big flat rock?

Upper Jay lies south of Jay. That's upstream, as the Ausable flows. The map pinpoints the location of the Land of Make Believe, one of the early theme parks, at the entrance to Upper Jay. Has the Land of Make Believe gone the way of the nail factory at Ferrona? Only an attractive brick building remains in the field, if indeed this was the site of the park.

The townspeople would know, but no one's around—except the kids skating by on skis equipped with wheels. Imagine chasing a gang of kids on road skis shouting: "Is this the Land of Make Believe?"

VISIT THE OLDEST GENERAL STORE IN THE NORTH COUNTRY says the sign on the large building at the corner. It is vacant. But the post office is open. So is the Old Seed Store across the street where a young couple inspect a display of wicker furniture. Upper Jay, too, leads the quiet life. You can fish from the bridge and not be disturbed. Except for the ski traffic.

Tourists again take over at Keene. Cars, campers and motorcycles claim the road. A few stop here, but for most, Keene is a milepost en route to Lake Placid. Two young men sit on the steps of the liquor store, sipping paper cartons of milk. Nearby is their motorcycle. Four kids push and shove their way from a van to the Keene Cream Machine. Their parents soon join them, reluctantly.

"Eat it all before you get back in the van," counsels Mother. "And don't forget to wipe your hands."

"Lookit that old snowmachine on the roof," said one of the kids, pointing to the Elm Tree Inn across the street.

"Geez…how long has it been there?" asked his younger brother.

"See the date…1824."

"Can't be that old."

Keene has been making its living from vacationers for a long time. No doubt the pace was easier when people came by stagecoach or horse and buggy and stayed for the summer—not just long enough to drink some milk or eat an ice cream cone.

Now the fire siren whines and southbound traffic stops. Quickly two men race from the firebarn and across the street where two cars have collided. One serves as traffic coordinator while the other tugs on a jammed door. They work like they've done it before. Soon the driver of the second car is out and traffic again moves up the hill and past North

Country Taxidermy and Trading Post where a stuffed bear is perched on a stump. Maybe the driver of that car in the accident suddenly slowed to take another look at the bear? Getting through Keene can be an adventure.

Keene Valley appears more relaxed, of another era. Sure enough, a Model A chugs into a motor court like it's still 1933—except now the place is called a motel, and the office in front has become a convenience store. But the trim overnight cottages are much the same. You still can park a step or two from your little house. A minute or two later you're unpacked and relaxed in your Adirondack chair. Not bad for an old place.

The same can be said for all of Keene Valley. It wears its age well, like that elderly lady under the broad-brimmed hat crossing from the Congregational Church to the library. Old-fashioned, shaded—still going strong.

Many of the High Peaks including Mt. Marcy, the highest of them all, are located within the Town of Keene. Some people come here to view the scenery, others to tackle it. Here you will find a quiet inn and a hiker's lodge, a store for those who scale mountains and another for those who paint them. Keene Valley caters to both.

St. Huberts puts you still closer to the High Peaks. The Ausable Club is located in a majestic frame structure dating from 1887. Its rambling porches offer spectacular views of the surrounding mountains.

So does the golf course...though one aspiring sport has hill enough before him on the fairway. He swings and misses. A practice swing perhaps? Again he addresses the ball and swings mightily. It dribbles a few feet. The green atop his hill looms high, unconquerable. Mountaineering might be easier.

For the hikers returning this afternoon, Marcy is more than a pretty view from porch and fairway. It is aching muscles, sore feet, tired bodies. So what if backpacks are a tangle of dirty socks and towels, or the final meal on the Coleman somewhat less than gourmet? Who cares? They've done it! Climbed the big one! Youthful enthusiasm quickly overflows the trailhead—spilling onto fairways, porches and beyond...

To the cooling waters

of Chapel Pond.

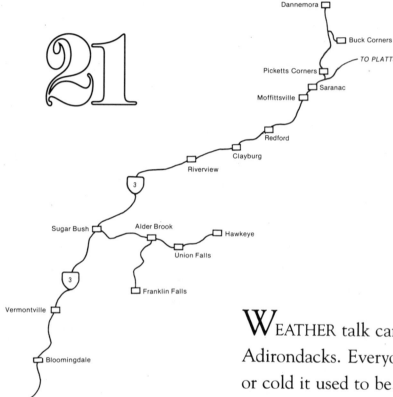

Dannemora

Buck Corners

TO PLATTSBURG

Picketts Corners

Saranac

Moffittsville

Redford

Clayburg

Riverview

3

Sugar Bush

Alder Brook

Hawkeye

Union Falls

3

Franklin Falls

Vermontville

Bloomingdale

TO SARANAC LAKE

21

BLOOMINGDALE, VERMONTVILLE, SUGAR BUSH, ALDER BROOK, FRANKLIN FALLS, UNION FALLS, HAWKEYE, RIVERVIEW, CLAYBURG, REDFORD, MOFFITTSVILLE, SARANAC, PICKETTS CORNERS, BUCK CORNERS, DANNEMORA

WEATHER talk can assume heroic dimensions in the Adirondacks. Everyone, it seems, has memories of how hot or cold it used to be. The year of no summer. Or no winter. The time wells ran dry and forest fires flared. Mountain weather is subject without end.

194

Chances are, the heat of this August day will soon be forgotten. Still, by midmorning you feel a tingle on your arm as you head north from Saranac Lake. Haze already dims McKenzie and the hills to the east. The day grows hotter.

At the Agway in Bloomingdale, they're comparing thermometers. "It's 80 at our place...that's in the shade."

"Mine says 83 on the milk shed."

"B-r-r-r-r."

Why not make fun of the weather? Can't do much about it anyway. Besides, it gives you something to laugh at in November when the plow goes on the pickup and the wind kicks snow across the driveway. But that's a long way off. Right now there's feed to load and groceries to pick up at Norman's.

Just about everyone goes to Norman's General Store when they're in town. It suits Bloomingdale about right—small enough to find what you're looking for, large enough to move around without bumping into a display. Not like the mall stores all cut from the same mold. Norman's has sparkling wood floors and walls to let you know it's been around a while—and cared for, too. Here's what a store used to be, I thought, reaching for a jar of honey.

"That comes from a teacher in Saranac who keeps bees in the

summer," said the man behind the counter. "We take all they make... about 140 pounds this year."

Then the phone rang, which gave me a chance to look for a few more items.

"How's his arm doing now?" asked the proprietor, relighting his corncob. "OK...two dozen regular...OK...OK...both sizes."

When was I last in a grocery store that took phone orders? The conversation continued item for item—a mix of groceries and news. You soon get the idea Norman's is more than a grocery store. PROVISIONERS AND OUTFITTERS SINCE 1904 the sign out front says. Sounds like a place you'd stock up the mule train for a trip west. Or an Apache camper headed for Buck Pond.

The Adirondacks' first airplane was said to have landed in a wheat field at Fletcher's farm, outside Bloomingdale.

"Probably up on Norman Ridge," said the proprietor. "The plateau's about the only place you could land in one piece."

His directions were perfect...a left turn at the old farmhouse to the top of the hill. There on a level stretch was a field of wheat, ready for cutting. Could this possibly be the field where the plane had landed, seventy-five harvests later? I found it hard to believe things hadn't changed—that the field was not brush and trees, or a dozen ranch houses.

196

What was it like that October twilight in 1912? By then the wheat had been harvested of course, making the field a perfect place to land. First you'd hear it...the faint droning of an engine. Something special you knew, for this sound was different. Next you'd spot a speck in the sky caught by the day's final rays as it circled the rim of Whiteface...gradually growing larger and larger as it neared the ridge. An aeroplane! Yes...and coming in right here! Then in disbelief you watch as the sputtering Burgess-Wright biplane plops onto the field, bouncing up and down, finally rolling to a stop. Ready or not, the age of flying machines had reached the Adirondacks.

Today, the field of wheat waves slightly in the warm breeze. Little has changed along this fertile ridge. Man still tills, plants, harvests. Swallows still dip and rise to the chase of insects—their flight surer, more graceful than man's could ever be.

Vermontville lays claim to more real estate along the highway than commerce requires. But that's one of the advantages of living in Vermontville. You can stretch out, breathe deep, and still get to the store in a minute or two. Might as well get the mail, too—along with the latest comings and goings. Even when the mail is all bulk rate, the comings and goings sometimes are first class.

But not all wags are at the post office this morning. Down the street, a friendly dog gives chase to a car turning onto the side road. Quickly, two kids bounce off a porch in pursuit of the dog, followed by a second dog in pursuit of the kids. Soon the excitement of the chase ended, and all return to await the next car which dares invade Vermontville's side road.

Sometimes maps and highway markers disagree. Not that it makes much difference at Sugar Bush, alias Merrills Corners. There's little here by any name other than a few houses at the corner and the Pinegrove Restaurant and Bar, whose patrons have come by car, pickup and logging truck.

Alder Brook doesn't make the map, period. Even so, a hand-lettered sign at St. Rose's Cemetery says "Alderbrook, NY Founded 1854." The Alder Brook flows nearby, and a posted area down the road is called Alder Brook Park. I was told that Father O'Donnell, who perished in a fire which destroyed his church, is buried on the site where the altar had stood.

Years ago, Franklin Falls was a bustling community with sawmill and forge. In those days the stage would stop at the hotel for dinner en route to Saranac Lake. Now the bumpy road passes only a stone fence hidden by brush and trees—heading nowhere beyond a steep hill. Franklin Falls is best remembered by its past.

At Union Falls, a man relaxes on his front porch, making guitar music. This looks like a place where you can sit and strum all day. Maybe listen to the music of the water flowing over the dam and falls. Or lean back in the boat, sip a beer, pretend you're fishing. No one's going to check your catch, even at McIntyre's fishing camp. Union Falls has no limit on loafing—especially on a hot day.

Silver Lake at Hawkeye is another good place to be, even when the breeze blows warm off the lake. You can still have fun belly flopping in the shallow water while Mom sets up the picnic and chases paper plates that have blown off the table. So what if haze starts to hide the south ridge, or if the lady at the beach house has to turn on the ceiling fan. "Maybe the fan doesn't fit the antique decor here," she said with a wry smile. "But in another hundred years who'll know the difference?"

Something about this place puts you back in time. Maybe the old pictures on the walls, or the tribute to the woman's late husband above the mantle. Or the building itself.

"This business has been going since 1860," she said. "Always in the same family, too. That's the original lodge over there."

She pointed to a building across the road. A wraparound second floor porch was the only giveaway of its age. Who would ever suspect this sturdy structure dates from Civil War days?

"We used to have a hotel across the street, too, but it was destroyed by fire," recalled the woman. Then she told how fire also had leveled their hotel in Ausable Forks in 1975. Tragically, that fire also took the life of her husband.

These days the business includes a number of housekeeping rentals and campsites around the lake. Others in the family help, including her granddaughter who came in with a load of ice for the freezer. Moments later the girl was cleaning a window.

"She's a big help," said Grandmother with obvious pride. "So are my grandsons."

Across the lake is Douglas Mountain, dimmed by the àfternoon haze. But it will be there tomorrow. So, it seems, will Douglas Camps and Campsites.

Most cars flow through the little settlements along Route 3 like water through the Saranac—twisting, turning, stopping not. You can pass through some of these places without realizing you've been there.

Riverview is typical. It has no official beginning or end. And little in between other than Mazzotte's General Store, where a biker has stopped for an equipment repair. Soon he is on his way, leaving vegetable gardens and woodpiles behind—passing what remains of Charles Beauchemin's General Store and Riverview's once-upon-a-time post office.

Over at the Clayburg Hotel they're saying it's too hot to work this afternoon. But the two men replacing shingles on the side of the hotel didn't get the message. Neither did the man painting trim up the street nor the woman next door who's hanging out wash. Guess Clayburg's no different from any other place. Some people spend the day working. And some spend the day talking about why they're not working.

Traffic starts to build behind a double-wide mobile home passing through Redford. The men on the porch of the Sportsman's Hotel watch the procession. This is as close as you get to a traffic jam in Redford.

The town has some surprises. The cemetery is larger than you might expect. So's the Catholic Church sitting on the hill, and the modern church school behind it.

At Jenny's Drive-In, the two boys with double-dip cones are in a race with the afternoon sun. This day takes extra napkins, but the boys finally prevail. So do the cars which had been trailing the double-wide now pulling into Jenny's. Quickly they pick up speed, escaping Redford.

Moffittsville comes and goes with a wipe of the brow. The River Run Restaurant posts a varied menu alongside its second sign: CLOSED.

Parked pickups, cars and a pulp truck tell you the Hi-Falls Lounge is the place to be in Saranac this afternoon. Just one car is parked at the town hall. Who wants to do business on a hot day?

Or who would pick this day to move out of an apartment? Apparently the couple down the road have no choice. First come boxes, suitcase, lamp, folding table and a TV which fit nicely into the trunk and back of their big old '73 Olds. Next a sofa and stuffed chair...no doubt destined for the auction gallery next door. Nope. They're roped to the roof. The Olds sinks lower. Finally a refrigerator appears, and across the trunk it goes. Now rear wheels all but disappear within rusted body. If that car could utter but one word, most certainly it would be "UNCLE!" Mercifully, the refrigerator is removed and set aside for another trip. After all, there's a limit even to what a '73 Olds can take.

Around Saranac a plaid shirt and feed cap is the uniform of choice—especially when you're headed for the feed store.

"How come you're in town today?" asked Mr. Red Plaid.

"Same as you," answered Mr. Blue Plaid. "When they need feed, you get it."

You don't see many kids hanging around Picketts Corners today. They're over at the park in the pool. So are some Moms and Dads. Why not? It's a great facility the Town of Saranac has built on the hill. Not just a pool, either...but a tennis court, basketball court, ball field, playground as well. Plus a view of the rolling farmland below.

The map says Buck Corners is up the road. Maybe it's the corner with a few houses, some junk cars—and a pretty view of the valley? But I found no road sign. Guess not many strangers come this way. That's just as well. They'd only complain about the grass growing high and the trim needing paint. They'd miss the whole point of why some people would rather live off the beaten path.

Where is Dannemora's prison? Entering town from the south, you see nothing out of the ordinary…here and there a swing set or wading pool…an elderly lady walking along with a bag of groceries…a child and mother returning books to the library.

But turn the corner. Suddenly massive walls and guard towers loom above Dannemora's shops and stores. You're not quite ready for it—a maximum security prison casting its shadow over Ting's Bar, Pearl's Department Store, the motel and—practically all downtown.

Still, Dannemora's residents are not concerned. The woman casually crossing the street with a dog on leash glances not at prison walls. Nor does the man entering the coffee shop with a basket of clothes. Dannemora's Lilliputians appear comfortable with their stone-faced Gulliver.

In fact, they're lucky to have this giant. Other places in the Adirondacks see industries come and go, hillsides gouged and abandoned, tourists gone with the leaves of fall. Not so with Dannemora's visitors. They're here for an extended stay.

PEASLEEVILLE
DEVINS CORNERS
HIGH BANK
STANDISH
LYON MOUNTAIN
LEDGER CORNERS
JERUSALEM
ALDER BEND
LORD CORNERS
HAMMOND CORNERS
ELLENBURG CENTER
THE FORGE
BRAINARDSVILLE
BELLMONT CENTER
MERRILL

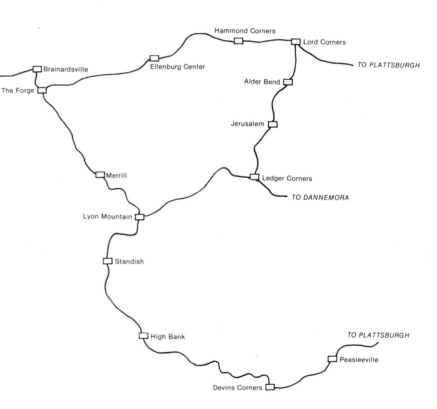

NOT many Adirondack visitors take the back roads. Too bad, for these twisting one-laners can put you in touch with some of the prettiest scenery the mountains have to offer—and some settlements you won't find on most maps.

Sure, you'll see the dead cars, appliances and other discards...the toys and bikes hiding in tall grass...fences doubled over with age, and neglect. Living gets more relaxed when you don't have the Joneses next door.

Peasleeville also has attractive homes, along with the Zion United Methodist Church and a Community Hall which might have been a schoolhouse in years past. I've been told fishing is good on the Salmon River, and Macomb State Park is but a few miles away. Still, not many people come this way, if only to pass through. At least I paused at roadside long enough to enjoy the expanse of tree-lined hills

to the south. You have a pleasant view from your window, Peasleeville.

Parking is no problem at Devins Corners. Just pull over to the field of goldenrod next to the ranch house of the same color. It's at the intersection of Ore Bed and Guide Board Roads. A few houses are here, along with a German police dog that wags rather than barks. That's the kind of dog to meet on a back road.

Why would an isolated settlement along a flat stretch be called High Bank? Maybe the stream which passes nearby has high banks? Or was the original settlement located back on the hill where an old schoolhouse still stands? One thing's for sure: the person who now farms this strip has a view stretching to the next county.

Last night's storm washed away the haze and oppressive heat. Now the highway crew is back with roller and trucks, giving Standish Road a new lease on life and passing cars a jingling of loose gravel.

Of course, when you're on Standish Road you expect to find Standish. Sure enough, here it comes…an attractive church called St. Michaels…a few houses and substation of the Saranac Fire Department…and there it goes.

Standish has no general store. You drive a few miles to get a loaf of bread. On the other hand, you can walk to the corner and pick a bouquet of field flowers. In some places, you don't live by bread alone.

Lyon Mountain is both hamlet and peak. The mountain Lyon is the highest in the northern Adirondacks, rising to a height of 3830 feet. Still, it is Lyon Mountain's slag pile which dominates the community's landscape—a towering reminder of its mining past. The old man leaning on his hoe needed no reminding. He knows what happened when the mine closed.

"Some of the younger people left to work the Republic mine in Witherbee. We older ones...you might say we retired...sometimes before we were ready to spend our time weeding."

These days some of the townspeople drive to Malone or other places out of the Park for work. Others are prison guards at Dannemora or at the correctional facility here in Lyon Mountain.

"The kids used to call the school a prison," chuckled the old man. "Funny how things turned out. It actually became a prison!"

Up the street, a furniture truck from Chateaugay stopped in front of a house while its driver surveyed the best way to reach the porch. Then, cautiously, he backed through driveway and yard—avoiding motorcycles, pickup and car parts in his path.

The slag pile still has its use. Three-wheeler tracks rise and dip endlessly along its steep slope. Here, too, a car lies buried to the hubcaps—abandoned like the pile which claims it.

Still, Lyon Mountain has color. Goldenrod and wild carrot in the fields…hollyhocks and roses at a side garden…spires of gladiola rising corn-high in a backyard patch. Nearly every house is bright with flowers. The community goes out of its way to make up for the colorless slag.

Language can grow colorful, too.

"Get outta there you *!%# mutt!" yelled the woman from atop a ladder where she was patching the roof. She had just spotted her dog as it rolled into the vegetable patch. The dog took no heed.

"GET OUT YOU !#$%&*!" This time she punctuated her annoyance with a toss of the tar stick.

Of course, a playful dog likes nothing better than a game of catch. Quickly it ran off with the tarred stick—straight through the line of freshly hung wash.

"Come back you *&%$#! mutt…COME BACK!" screamed the woman as the dog pranced in glee—her words falling on floppy deaf ears, bent tomatoes and a slightly tarred wash.

Lyon Mountain's old train station shows a sign for the post office above the back door, and the familiar faces of the Bartles and Jaymes advertising characters at the window. But the door to ZIP 12952 is locked, the post office empty except for this point-of-purchase display.

Now the strains of country music flow from Greg's Tavern at the

208

other side of the station. Greg's is open for business alright, but no cars are in front, and no customers within. Guess Ed Bartles and Mr. Jaymes will have to sip wine coolers by themselves, for a while at least.

You know when it's noon in Lyon Mountain. Gongs and bells echo from the church and correctional facility. Moments later, the fire department's siren joins the chorus. No reason to be late for lunch here.

Chazy Lake sparkles in the noonday sun. Above, puffy clouds relax...in no hurry to get on with their day. Soon a young couple from Quebec select a remote stretch off the road for an impromptu swim and picnic...in no hurry to get on with their day, either.

Fields and meadows checkerboard the valley between Topknot and Dannemora Mountains. Ledger Corners may have been more when Plank Road was but a plank road. Even if there's no sign here, the driver of the Frito Lay delivery truck stopping at the corner store knows where he is.

Jerusalem is on Alder Bend Road, starting at the RABBIT CROSSING sign and ending at BEWARE OF DOG. Here you can hang out deer horns as well as the wash. Or let the goldenrod grow right to the doorstep. Who cares? You can even go down the road to Jericho without the walls tumbling down.

Alder Bend has a settlement marker! Or is it the Alder Bend road

marker that's been turned around? Either way, you know where you are, next to the farm with a FOR SALE sign. Further along is more activity…an elderly man mowing his lawn…a girl crossing the road to pick up today's mail…kids tiptoeing along a rocky streambed.

Lord Corners is well-named, but nonoccupied—at least for now. Once there was a store at the intersection, I understand. Today there is only a cornfield. Some places are better suited for corn than commerce.

The greenhouse near Hammond Corners is built to take North Country winters. It appears more a fortress than plant shelter. This edge of the park belongs to the St. Lawrence Valley. The road runs straight and flat—past fields of goldenrod and ragweed.

Ellenburg Center is one of few farm communities within the Park. The mountains and woods lie to the south. Here, rocky pastures, cow corn, and dairy farms dot the landscape—a reminder you're still in the St. Lawrence Valley. Here, too, cows huddle under the big maple at a hedgerow, swallows tag a fresh hatch of insects above the cornfield, and a shockless Ford raises dust as it bounces along.

Down the road you spot a BINGO sign—at the Methodist Church it seems. Can this be so? Bingo at the Methodist Church? Correction…the sign is posted next door—at the fire department. Whew!

"There's no bingo at the Methodist Church…for sure," said one of

the road sweepers at the town hall. He smiled at the thought of a stranger misplacing the fire department sign. "Used to have movies, though… right here in the hall. But now it's just the town offices and library."

Everyone waves around here, even the farmer who pulled his tractor to the side of the road. You get the idea just about every car in the territory is known. When a strange vehicle appears, it's an event of sorts. You wave back. These are people you somehow know.

"Bet you're lost," shouted the man from a riding mower.

"Nope," I replied proudly. "This is The Forge, right?" He seemed surprised someone knew the name of his corner. But soon my true ignorance was discovered.

"Where's the forge located?"

"Haven't had one for about a hundred years. Turn down the road to the dam. But there's no sign of it."

Actually, there are signs—for Kiln Road, and Blow Road where the Seventh Day Adventist Church stands. These names are dead giveaways of the past. There's another sign, too…the historical marker on the corner which reports the world's largest catalan forge was here, built in 1874 and abandoned in 1893.

Today, a mobile home is at the dam, and water turns murky in the pond below. Looks like a place you could fish…with plenty of time

between bites to figure out why the world's largest catalan forge lasted only nineteen years.

Brainardsville has a few stores and its own post office. It also has a beagle limping along the road in no special hurry. That's alright. No traffic along here, anyway.

Bellmont Center takes up a lot of real estate for a few houses and Legacy's Groceries. Enough space here for a city. But that's looking ahead.

"A tourist...huh?" guessed the friendly lady at the store. "We don't get many this way. Maybe a few when the fair's on."

Mountain roads are named for about anything. On the other side of Lower Chateaugay, beyond the cattails, is W. P. A. Road. No doubt quite a few roads were built by the W. P. A.

Merrill's general store handles the summer trade around Upper Chateaugay Lake. Nearby is a liquor and hardware store. They appear to share the same entrance.

"Sure you can swim in the lake," said the woman carrying a bag of groceries. "Just down the road past Bob Merrill's woodworking shop."

Never was a mountain lake more inviting. Now a gentle breeze wrinkled the cool waters of the sandy bay where children frolicked and a sailboat bobbed. On a day like this, you could grab a cloud and float forever. At least to Labor Day.

"A gentle breeze
wrinkled the cool
waters of the
sandy bay."

213

23

**DEERLAND
LONG LAKE
SABATTIS
NEWCOMB
WINEBROOK
TAHAWUS
ADIRONDAC**

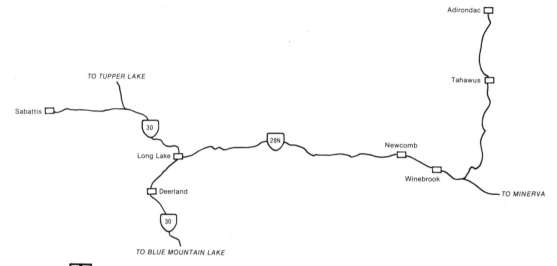

THERE'S a little settlement at a bend in the road on Route 30 that gets my vote for the most fanciful name in the Adirondacks—Deerland. Mention it and I picture a highland glade in the shadow of the forest where does graze and fawns frolic. Bambi would be happy to live in Deerland.

Deerhead, another bend in the road along Route 9, conjures no such thoughts. Deerhead is just a trophy on the wall. You'd think more places in the Adirondacks would be named for the wildlife. Owls Head in Franklin County is named for a rock formation. Big Moose was named for a species which disappeared from the Adirondacks for a century. Perhaps they'll both make a comeback. The beaver have come back, better than Beaver River in fact. Too bad no road goes to Beaver River. Beartown in Warren County does have a road but hardly anyone takes it. Nothing's there but a turnaround, and maybe a bear or two.

Deerland, however, has houses, camps, and plenty of traffic—especially in summer. A place with a name this delightful should have its own highway sign, and perhaps a petting deer or two.

"Deerland had a sign," said the man at the turnoff to Buttermilk Falls. "But someone knocked it down about twenty-five years ago."

"Too bad it wasn't put up again."

"Why? People here know it's Deerland. We had a post office, too. It's still in storage down the road."

Who wouldn't welcome a letter with that postmark?

Actually, Deerland has petting deer—three fawns in the care of the area's own wildlife rehabilitator. The young animals appeared nervous at the sight of a stranger. "You can sense when they're ready to go," said their caretaker. "Any day now for these two."

Within seconds the fawns had emptied their bottles. Afterwards, one approached cautiously, then licked my hand. Disney didn't exaggerate when he drew those eyes and eyebrows! Guess this was the first time I had petted a deer.

"They seem so tame. Are you sure they're ready for the woods?"

"If I were to open this door they'd be gone. Believe me, their wildness is always there."

"Don't you worry about them? Don't you wonder if a hunter will get that buck some day?"

"They leave healthy…and have a good chance of survival. That's the best anyone can do."

In addition to deer, the wildlife rehabilitator has cared for loons, great blue herons, a variety of small birds, racoons, and a coyote…all orphaned or injured when brought to her by State Conservation Officers. Her photo album is filled with pictures and penned comments. A smile comes to her face as she recalls a particular one. Quite a family of wildlife.

Friends came to see the baby golden racoon, little more than a small brown bundle in her arms. The cat cast a wary eye, but didn't budge from its chair.

"The racoon is blind," explained its surrogate Mother, "…and has other problems, too. But it calms down as soon as you feed it."

Sure enough. The racoon soon snuggled in her arms, as content as any baby could be. It was like something you'd see on Mr. Rogers, or read in a storybook. I wouldn't have been surprised to see Uncle Wiggly hopping down from Buttermilk Falls. Sugar Plum Island had to be nearby, too.

Long Lake is actually a wide stretch of the Raquette River. Early explorers accurately called it "Wide River." But because this thirteen-mile section has the appearance of a lake, it came to be called Long Lake. The outpost which developed along the shoreline took this name as well. The lake and associated waterway were its lifeline to the outside world.

Those who paddled this disjointed network of streams and lakes soon realized their need for a boat which was strong yet light in weight—one uniquely suited to mountain waters and carries. The boats built by local guides using native cedar quickly became the standard for water travel throughout the region. These days, Adirondack guideboats are prized by collectors. A few are still in use. On Long Lake, however, outboards and airplanes have taken over.

This late summer afternoon, the blue plane of Helms Aero Service taxied to its mooring near the beach where three passengers climbed out. They've just returned from a bird's-eye view of lakes and mountains not soon forgotten. An outboard skimmed past the beach.

217

"When does soccer start?" shouted a boy passing on his bike.

"Next week I think," answered the lifeguard.

September has a way of sneaking up. Just a couple of weeks before people here were sweltering, and the beach was full. Now the leaves are turning, a cool breeze blows down the lake, and the kids already are talking soccer.

Still, every store in town seems busy—from Northern Borne to Hoss's Country Corner. Thank goodness. The quiet season starts soon, and lasts long. The kids sitting on the steps at Adirondack Outfitters know. Already they're talking about who's going to roll up the sidewalks and where they'll be stored. Every year the kids have fun joking about the sidewalks. Just like their dads and moms used to do. Not much changes in Long Lake.

Maybe that's why people still talk about Sabattis in the present tense. "That's out by Sabattis," someone might say. Sure enough, a state mileage marker points the way in from Route 30. And what do you find? A decaying train station, the rusty tracks of the old Adirondack Railway—and memories.

Once Sabattis had a post office, hotel, electric power plant, store, lumberyard, schoolhouse—and a livery which held as many as 200 horses. It was eighteen miles to Long Lake—as close as the railroad would come to the lakeside community. With a sense of civic pride, some called the new settlement Long Lake West. By any name, its future appeared bright.

Then in 1903, fire swept through the new railroad community. Several hundred pounds of dynamite exploded during the fire, and the settlement was demolished. In time, Sabattis was rebuilt, but its eventual fate was sealed as automobile travel grew increasingly popular.

These days Sabattis Road has little traffic other than an occasional sportsman or Boy Scouts from the Onondaga Council headed to their campsite, Camp Sabattis. No doubt those who first scouted Long Lake, Peter and Mitchell Sabattis, would be pleased today's scouts honor their memory.

Route 28N is Newcomb's Main Street. The town hall, school and most of its houses are here. The place hangs on the edge of the woods. The Huntington Wildlife Forest Station just west of town is the site of the satellite Adirondack Interpretive Center at Rich Lake. To the south lies Goodnow Flow, its streams, lakes and hills a favorite for fishing and hunting. And just to the north is the Santanoni Preserve—over 200 square miles of prime Adirondack woodland, and a network of trails.

"I'm headed for Moose Pond," said a hiker pulling into the trailhead. "Maybe to Cold River where Rondeau had his camp."

The town park at Harris Lake is cold, empty today. Briefly, a kingfisher chatters from a limb overhanging the water. Then all was quiet. Newcomb's solitude nurtures the hermit lingering somewhere in all of us.

Winebrook looks as though it moved here from the suburbs. That's half right. The community actually was moved—not from the suburbs, however, but from a nearby mining community. Some years ago, National Lead Company uprooted Tahawus and moved it—lock, stock and churches—to a new site east of Newcomb...thus opening up new land for the Company's mining operations.

"That was some sight," recalled the woman at the Winebrook Market. "Imagine a whole town rolling down the road. The company wrote it up and gave pictures to employees and the people in town."

"Did it go smoothly?"

"Just like clockwork. Everyone was moved in by Christmas. But after all that, they're closing the mine."

This area has had its ups and downs before. The original mine which had prospered for a number of years was closed in the mid-nineteenth century. The mine remained dormant until World War II when National Lead Company started titanium production.

"Now our only newcomers are retired people moving up from the city," said the woman. "Sure hope the school doesn't close, too."

Tahawus is Indian for "He splits the sky." Mt. Marcy, the highest peak in the state, was first given this name. The community which grew around the nearby mine later adopted the name for its own. These days, only a deep hole remains where Tahawus had stood. Did the Indians have a word for "He splits the ground?"

A crew is busy demolishing the administration building.

"Back in the fifties, 400 worked here," said the man with a crowbar. "Now it's 38...and dropping. There's no more mining. Just selling off the slag."

"Is this the post office you're tearing down?"

"Just the front is the post office. Zip 12879 is about to go."

I sensed history in the making—or rather, in the razing.

"Here...let me get a final picture of ole 12879."

Quickly, the crew caught the spirit of the occasion.

"Wait a minute," said one, reclaiming a letter box from the debris on the floor. It fit perfectly between two wall studs. "How's this?" he asked.

"Hold it," I replied, snapping the shutter.

"Gangway!" yelled someone on the roof. Hunks of shingles and boards thumped as they landed.

"See that pine tree?" asked another, pointing to a distant tree on the opposite side of the excavation. It stood alone on the hillside.

"That was where the Plant Superintendent lived. The fireplace in his backyard is still there."

Maybe the fireplace is going to be the only thing left in Tahawus. Except the hole.

Along the road to Adirondac is the old slag pile where brush and alder have taken root. Already Nature has started its slow, deliberate process of reclaiming the area. Brush grows on the old MacIntyre blast furnace, too—its chimney a monument to the early iron mine in the area. Beyond are the decaying houses of Adirondac.

At the trailhead to the High Peaks, a notice on the bulletin board warns hikers not to drink stream water—a source of beaver fever.

"Is this Saturday?" asked a returning hiker. He still looked healthy enough. "You kinda lose track of time out there."

Could time-disorientation be a symptom of beaver fever? I assured him this day was Saturday.

"It's beautiful back at Duck Hole," he exclaimed. "Didn't take long at all to get the tent up in the thunderstorm. Once I got inside, and the flannel dried, I stopped shivering, too."

No beaver fever for sure. Just hiker enthusiasm.

"That must be great," I said, "surviving with what's on your back."

Somehow, my words didn't sound very convincing.

"Beyond are the
decaying houses
of Adirondac."

24

**WAWBEEK, SARANAC INN,
LAKE CLEAR/JUNCTION,
PAUL SMITHS, GABRIELS,
HARRIETTSTOWN,
RAINBOW LAKE, ONCHIOTA,
LOON LAKE, WALKER MILL,
MOUNTAIN VIEW, OWLS HEAD,
DUANE CENTER, McCOLLOMS**

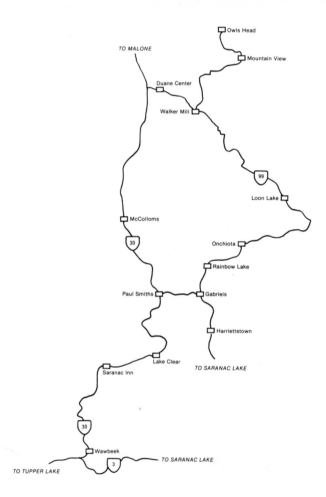

EARLY fall is the season for leaf peekers and bear hunters. Hikers and campers, too—for a short summer dies hard in the Adirondacks. Yet who can deny change is in the air?

Certainly not the ladies in sensible shoes who come from Albany to savor autumn's first flush and the quiet of the hills. Nor the hunters who set up camp along Dump Road, seeking bear, bar—and breakfast at the diner, where a NO GUNS OR KNIVES sign greets customers. Hardly a place for quiche, the Albany ladies decide even before they see the menu.

Family campers are here as well, looking like a page from L.L. Bean—stretching summer one last weekend. Still, fall is everywhere. Gone are the gentle breezes of July and August from the Upper Saranac. Now skies darken, winds blow raw, and leaves drift against the empty cottages at

Wawbeek. Only the caretaker remains. Only the sound of hammer and saw from across the bay disturbs the quiet of this day. A summer place that's out of summer gets lonely in a hurry.

Traffic is heavy along the Saranacs this weekend. Campers head for Fish Creek, leaf peekers push further north, and students from Quebec load their canoes at Hickok's Boat Livery. Isn't Saranac Inn nearby?

"Take the next turnoff," said the elderly biker. "You'll see the golf course and motel."

Somehow I expected Saranac Inn to be a rambling old place with a wraparound porch and people in rocking chairs. Maybe that's what it used to be. The biker was right. The place is a golf course and motel. The inn is only a memory.

Suddenly this dark day sprung a leak. Then drizzle turned to sleet. Still golfers arrive, and boaters back their trailers to water's edge. It's going to take more than a dismal weekend to shut down summer at Saranac Inn—even if most cottages had their last hurrah on Labor Day.

Lake Clear is hamlet, lake—and Junction where the train once stopped. These days Lake Clear has the only airport within the Adirondack Park with scheduled passenger flights. Sure enough, a Piedmont commuter from Albany touches down, right on schedule, too. Quickly the door opens, and the pilot emerges with clipboard in hand, followed by two passengers. All three enter the frame terminal. Moments later the pilot returns to the plane, and the Piedmont Commuter again is airborne. No delays at Adirondack Airport.

Remember Lake Clear? It's the place with a pleasant name, post office on the corner and an attractive school further along. A few who head north this day might also recall the FLEA MARKET EVERY SATURDAY sign next to a parked van where blankets wave in the breeze.

Now drizzle turns to downpour and winds pick up. The blankets cling to their line for dear life as Lake Clear's Yankee peddler decides to pack up his flea market for this Saturday.

At Paul Smith's College, two students cross the rain-soaked green from dorm to Student Union. The day is hardly ideal for parents to visit. Yet who else would dash from dorm to car with newspaper-umbrellas above their heads? Certainly not the boy following behind. He's not about to run. A Blazer filled with kids slows as it passed.

"See you later in Saranac," hailed the driver.

The boy nodded, pointing toward his parents. The others understood. He'll see them later, after they leave. This is no day to study.

Not many colleges have a boat launch on campus. Nor an outdoor classroom of rustic benches overlooking lake and mountain. Paul Smith would be pleased how closely the college's hotel management and conser-

227

vation programs still mirror his lifelong interests—how well his Adirondack legacy endures.

A soft rain falls on a leaf-covered country churchyard at St. John of the Wilderness. Here a robin dances and listens...dances and listens. But a meal is not to be found. Soon this ground turns hard. Then the birds of summer are gone—seeking warmer rains, softer earth.

Where do you hang out in Gabriels on a wet day? Probably the St. Regis Inn where most of the cars are parked. Or maybe at Ted's Grocery down the street where a bareheaded young man leaves with a six-pack. He's set for an afternoon of TV football. You don't see many umbrellas in country places like Gabriels—even during a heavy rain. They seem more the tool of cities and suburbs.

The settlement at Harriettstown has a spattering of houses along one side of the road and an old cemetery overlooking the valley on the other side. The hills to the east have changed little from the day this ridge was first settled.

Why do the mapmakers spell Harriettstown with a single "T" when the town name above the entrance to the cemetery has "TT"? Those who did the ironwork must have known the correct spelling. Now if someone would only replace the "E" and the leg of the "N" missing from the sign, Harriettstown's good name would be completely restored.

Again the sun peeks through drizzle. But Rainbow Lake has no rainbow—only the lights of oncoming cars reflecting off the slick asphalt. At the Adirondack Swim and Trip Camp for Boys, a man removes limbs downed by the wind. A few seasonal homes also are located along this stretch. Here the lake and its elusive rainbow—if indeed there is one—are hidden.

Onchiota's post office also is hidden. But everything else about this little place is quite in view—especially the signs. Onchiota speaks sign language.

IF YOU CAN'T STOP, SMILE AS YOU PASS BY says one of them. I stopped and smiled, but saw no one. Just another sign at the Seven Gables Grocery: THE STORE WITH THREE WONDERS. YOU WONDER IF WE HAVE IT. WE WONDER WHERE IT IS. YOU WONDER HOW THE HELL WE FOUND IT. I tried the door at The Seven Gables Grocery. It was locked.

Then I spotted Onchiota's farewell sign: LEAVING 67 OF THE FRIENDLIEST PEOPLE IN THE ADIRONDACKS (PLUS A COUPLE OF SOREHEADS). You have to respect Onchiotaites. They tell it as it is.

Down the road is the Six-Nation Indian Museum. From the woods a shrill "caw-w-w caw-w-w" broke the silence.

"They're ravens," said the old man. "I feed them. Also feed the bears."

A bird somewhat larger than a crow swooped down from a tree, screeching.

"Boy, they sure make noise," I said. Then a Volkswagon minus muffler rattled past.

"I'd rather hear my birds than that," he answered, turning toward the woods.

The museum was closed, but I was invited to walk the grounds. Near the entrance was a plaque cut in the shape of a pelt. It offered a perspective of New York history by the Cayugan, Ha-A-Wa-No-Onk:

"The Empire State as you love to call it was once laced by our trails from Albany to Buffalo, trails that we had trod for centuries, trails worn so deep by the feet of the Iroquois League that they became your roads of travel. As your possessions gradually cut into those of my people your roads still traversed these same lines of communicaton which bound one part of the Long House to the other. Have we, the first holders of this prosperous region no longer a share in its history? Glad were your fathers to sit down upon the threshold of the Long House. Had our forefathers spurned you from it when the French were thundering at the opposite door to get a passage through and drive you into the sea, whatever had been the fate of other Indians, the Iroquois might still have been a Nation, and I, instead of pleading here for the privilege of living within your borders, I might have had a Country."

For a few minutes I walked still paths, passing displays of miniature teepees, fireplaces, totem poles. Then I stopped at a wishing well for the SAVE THE ANIMAL FUND. For sure the ravens and bears would benefit. Possibly the red squirrel, too, which had been following at a safe distance, watching my every move. "Plunk" went my coin as it hit the larger pan—joining pine needles in the bottom of the SAVE THE ANIMAL FUND.

Now steam rises from distant hills. At Loon Lake on the old Port Kent-Hopkinton turnpike, golfers quickly return to the fairways, and strollers to the private roadway winding past turn-of-the-century cottages and maples bright with fall.

Loon Lake is less inhabited than its namesake to the south. Perhaps some loons are here, though I saw none from the isolated road which traces its shoreline. Suddenly an animal crossed the road ahead— its movement far quicker than a dog. In a flash it disappeared into the woods. A young coyote no doubt.

Again the sun plays hide-and-seek. But clouds cannot shield

231

autumn's beauty from those who travel the narrow, twisting road to Duck Pond. Why hasten along this turnpike built for stage, not speed? Why not join birch, beech, maple in their brief celebration? Winter soon is with us.

Structures come and go in the Adirondacks, but names linger. Today nothing is left of Walker's old mill along the turnpike. Yet Walker Mill remains the name of this lonely stretch of red pine, moss and sandy soil—awaiting arrival of its next settler.

Further along, several attractive homes line the road.

"Is this Mountain View?" I asked the man on the riding mower.

"It's straight ahead."

"So what's this place called?"

"Nothing…just country."

Too bad. Walker Mill is a nonplace with a name, and here's a place with some fine homes and no name. Maybe it should be called Barnesville. My map shows a Barnes Brook nearby. And a Barnes Pinnacle. Every settlement deserves a name.

Not many people make it to Mountain View these days. Years ago when the train stopped, Mountain View had more visitors. You'd go to a place like Mountain View Lake or nearby Indian Lake and stay for a month or two—maybe the whole summer.

Today nothing is left of the railroad—just power lines and a snowmobile trail on its right-of-way. Whenever a strange vehicle rolls into town, you figure the driver has taken a wrong turn. Grown-ups peek out at you, and kids ask where you're going. Mountain View could use more visitors who haven't lost their way. After all, the mountain view is as pretty as ever.

Owls Head is a few miles north. WELCOME TO YOUR PLAYGROUND said the sign in a field. But the kids prefer to play in the road or the yard of Wood's Country Store across the street.

"How did Owls Head get that name?" I asked.

"See it smiling right over there?" replied a boy, pointing to a rock formation looming from a hill behind the playing field.

"The beak fell off, but the eyes and smile are still there. See it?"

I strained to see an owl. It looked more like a rock on a hill. Or maybe a man. But Man's Head wouldn't sound right. Owls Head is more a name the Indians would select.

"Yes…I see the owl," I finally replied.

Now two boys sped down the road on their little bikes, followed by several others. In some places you see more children than adults. That's eight bikers I counted—plus the kids in the yard at the store. And not a grown-up around. At least, none were in evidence.

What if the kids have taken over Owls Head—like something from "Twilight Zone?" See...there's even a couple more in the driveway up the street. Hold it! Someone's crawling out from under the car. Sure enough...an honest-to-goodness grease-covered father, complete with drip pan and wrench.

"Get outa that oil!" he yelled.

The kids flew into the house. Guess the grown-ups are still in charge of Owls Head.

You get the feeling Duane Center hasn't changed much. The old church, unoccupied and nameless, is still in reasonable condition. The former schoolhouse is now a dwelling. Yesterday's cars still find a home in some of the yards. If you come back years from now, Duane Center will be the same.

Along the road, a stand of young maples is ablaze with the colors of fall. The few houses of McColloms are separated by field, brush—and a cemetery with more headstones than you might suspect. Was McColloms a lumbering settlement before a forest fire swept the area?

As darkness descends, you stop to read the historical sign reporting this tragedy. Then a pickup speeds past, loaded with firewood. Quickly you are reminded that in this country of long winters, fire is also man's friend.

234

"...a stand
of young maples
is ablaze with
the colors of fall."

235

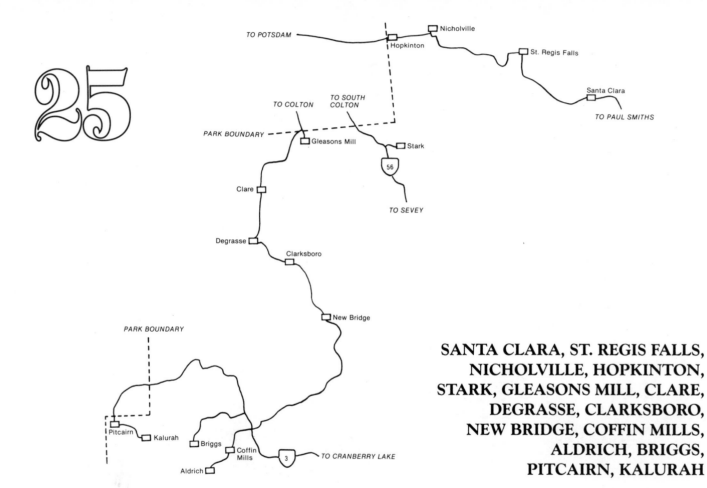

TO POTSDAM

Nicholville

Hopkinton

St. Regis Falls

Santa Clara

TO PAUL SMITHS

TO COLTON

TO SOUTH COLTON

PARK BOUNDARY

Gleasons Mill

Stark

56

Clare

Degrasse

TO SEVEY

Clarksboro

New Bridge

PARK BOUNDARY

Pitcairn

Kalurah

Briggs

Coffin Mills

3

TO CRANBERRY LAKE

Aldrich

SANTA CLARA, ST. REGIS FALLS, NICHOLVILLE, HOPKINTON, STARK, GLEASONS MILL, CLARE, DEGRASSE, CLARKSBORO, NEW BRIDGE, COFFIN MILLS, ALDRICH, BRIGGS, PITCAIRN, KALURAH

HOW quickly hardwoods pay their dues to October's rain and wind! By midmonth only a hint of red and yellow remain on northern hills. Autumn's fireworks are done. Now tamarack turns gold, and goldenrod turns brown. These are bonus days before snow flies—a time to breathe deep the cool fall air...to explore the woodland meadow where an aging monarch lingers and milkweed sheds its fleece. Time also to explore new roads to Santa Clara, St. Regis Falls...the edges of the Park.

Years ago, these hills were a wasteland of stumps. Trees again grow tall. A loaded pulp truck passes. Another harvest begins.

The highway skirts Santa Clara. Still, you see it all across the field—St. Peter's Catholic Church, a few houses and trailers, the concrete block building housing town hall

and garage. Santa Clara once was an outpost community along the railroad. Now it's an outpost community along the highway.

What's a pickup doing in town with a full load of apples? Santa Clara is not exactly apple country.

"They're culls from the orchard in Peru," the young man told me. "Go ahead. Pick'em over. What's left I feed to the pigs."

"How about the deer?" asked his friend who was filling up a paper bag.

The young man answered with a smile.

At noon, the siren calls St. Regis Falls to lunch. On cue, two cars pull into the Riverside Hotel and town trucks stop at the Eskimo Inn, a small geodetic dome up the street.

"You're open year 'round, aren't you?" asked a customer.

"This building's been here twenty-some years," replied the waitress. "I don't think it's ever been open in the winter. We're closing in November."

"I've never heard an igloo to close in the winter," joked the man putting on his jacket.

The guys in the town crew chuckled. Bet they'll miss the big cheeseburgers and french fries when Eskimo Inn closes for the winter.

The Town of Waverly park has already shut down. "But drive right in," the man said. The little park overlooking the falls has campsites and vacation cottages. Looks like a good place to visit in July or August. Certainly it's a delight on a day the playful breeze coaxes leftover leaves from a stubborn maple.

St. Regis Falls can't wait for Halloween. Already jack-o-lanterns peek from windows, corn shocks hug doorways, hobgoblins hang from clotheslines. Trick or treating promises to be something special.

So does Hunter's Breakfast the next morning. A sign near the fire department gives the full menu: scrambled eggs, sausage, bacon, pancakes/pure syrup, home fries, and pastries. You don't go deer hunting around St. Regis Falls on an empty stomach.

Near Nicholville, an old wooden fence zigzags through roadside brush and woods. Once this land had been pasture. Soon the fence returns to earth. Then a father might tell his child: "I used to climb a wooden fence along this road"

"Was there not a house and barn as well?" the child asks.

"Perhaps. But that was before my time."

How quickly history is lost.

Just about everything in Nicholville is old—the houses, stores, certainly the big maples. But on a sunny fall afternoon, old is beautiful—even if paint is not a best seller in town. Judging from the weathered signs

and exterior, it's been a while since the Masons or Eastern Star did ceremony in their building. A while, too, since the old building housing the post office has seen scraper or brush.

I greeted a bearded young man seated on a small porch next to the BEWARE OF DOG sign. But he did not answer. Perhaps the country music floating through the torn screen door was louder than my voice. Or maybe he doesn't have words for a stranger.

Nicholville looks inviting enough—especially the park where the old turnpike passes and the Highway Supervisor posts a sign for his reelection. From the bridge you see the St. Regis River racing by—unspoiled, untamed. Along a tree-lined street are attractive homes, a church, and Nicholville's own telephone company.

Who would guess a little farm community at the edge of the Park would have a museum/library, town offices, Congregational Church, and town hall—all surrounding a tree-studded village green? Hopkinton reminds you of a little place in Vermont, especially this fall afternoon when you spot the two boys raking a carpet of leaves into a mighty hill. Suddenly, one dove head first into the pile.

"Hey...we gotta finish," said his companion, speaking like a parent...then acting like a kid as he, too, leaped into the leaves.

"OK...OK," said the first boy, brushing himself off.

Jumping into a pile of leaves might just be the best thing about fall in Hopkinton—next to Halloween.

Hopkinton has been around long enough for the British to have invaded. That was in 1814 when they grabbed 300 barrels of flour from the barns of Colonel Hopkins. Currently, the only stock of flour in town is on the shelf of the convenience store. No sign of raiders either, though now and then a salesman might slip into town to write an order, and maybe stop at Sarah's Country Kitchen for a cup of coffee.

How come Stark made the map? Maybe because there's a blank spot in this remote area—with plenty of space to fit in a short name like Stark. Not much is here, other than a couple of houses near a country cemetery, the Niagara Mohawk power plant at Carry Falls Reservoir—and a big boulder along Route 56 that's about perfect for painting names. Just ask Dave B., Lynn N., Kathy K. and Kelly Q. of SUNY 87' (sic). Or those who came before and since with brush and bucket.

Somehow you sense the narrow road to Gleasons Mill leads neither to mill nor settlement—just to wild and pretty scenery. Yet surely that is reason enough to continue along this trail of white crushed stone, past yesterday's pastures and today's hunting camps...even when the music from Radio Tupper declares: "If Heaven ain't a lot like Dixie, I don't want to go." Each to his own, they say.

The 121 people living in the Town of Clare have plenty of stretching space. A few houses are scattered along the road where town building and airfield are located—but that's it. I couldn't find another road with power lines. Somewhere there are a hundred people more in Clare.

Country places can show more past than promise. Usually a new settlement will grow and prosper for a while. Then the mill it serves might close, or its mine shut down. The place no longer has reason to exist. Before long, only a shell remains.

Degrasse, which touches the western boundary of the Park, is one of yesterday's communities. No doubt, its maples were planted with love, nurtured with hope for the future. Now they are old, untended—sharing the roadside with unused buildings, unused cars. Towne's General Store and a convenience store stand at the edge of town, leaving the rest of Degrasse intact with its past.

Perhaps Clarksboro once had mines? Orebed Ponds and Orebed Swamp are in the area. But no power lines or buildings are here. Only the Grasse River meandering out of the Park.

New Bridge is just that, a new bridge...plus the concrete remains of the old bridge along a bumpy stretch of road with no warning markers. But then, most who come this way already are on a first-name basis with

242

the bumps. So you take your time bouncing along, enjoying the wild and rugged beauty…wondering why a little bridge would rate recognition on any map?

Some settlements are almost impossible to find. Coffin Mills has no marker. Maybe it's the place where a roof tilts earthward on a vacant building and a former school bus is parked at a house? You know these people are getting ready for winter. A log splitter is in the driveway, and storm windows lean against the bus. You know hunting season has arrived, too. Why else would so many pickups head this way?

Aldrich does have a sign: WELCOME TO ALDRICH. POP? SOME HEMLOCK, SOME SPRUCE, THE HOME OF ALDRICH FISH-GAME CLUB INC. Gangway! Down the road came a pickup kicking dust—a man, woman, and two kids stuffed in the cab, and barking dogs behind. Then two more pickups arrived. Suddenly, Aldrich's population was more than hemlock and spruce.

Is Briggs the settlement at Sucker Lake, or is it further along at the railroad tracks? No one is around to ask—except a fisherman who stays far out on the lake even when the wind grows mean, the sky darkens—and rain starts to fall.

Pitcairn is more hamlet than settlement. Several houses are here, along with a cemetery, a church which is being rebuilt, and town offices which double as a polling place on election day. But no people are out campaigning today.

Someone is out for a ride, however.

"Is this the road to Kalurah?" I asked the man at the corner of Jayville Road.

"Where?" he replied, driving on. Kalurah's not exactly on the tip of the tongue, even here.

So you wing it past a staging area for logging, a cottage along the stream with a footbridge—twisting your way to nowhere special. Is Kalurah near the tracks where a few houses stand? Who cares about the destination?

Some roads you take

simply for the pleasure

of the journey.

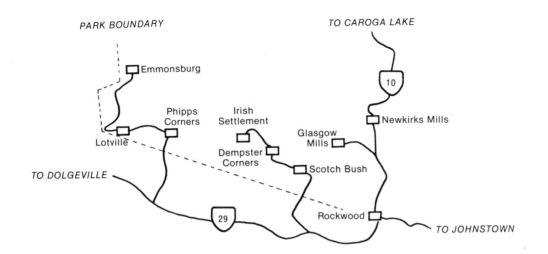

PARK BOUNDARY

TO CAROGA LAKE

Emmonsburg

Phipps
Corners

Irish
Settlement

10

Newkirks Mills

Lotville

Dempster
Corners

Glasgow
Mills

Scotch Bush

TO DOLGEVILLE

29

Rockwood

TO JOHNSTOWN

WHAT do you call that brief interval between frost and freeze—when the nip in the air is just right for hiking, the light cover of snow just right for tracking? Is this yet fall? Already wind blows cold and ice rims the pond. Or is this the start of winter?

November's days are often in limbo, a period between seasons when work outside is done—inside not begun. So

ROCKWOOD
GLASGOW MILLS
NEWKIRKS MILLS
SCOTCH BUSH
DEMPSTER CORNERS
IRISH SETTLEMENT
PHIPPS CORNERS
LOTVILLE
EMMONSBURG

what if skies threaten and winds chase chickadees to cover? The wood is split, storm windows on.

What better day to travel past the hunter's trailers and converted buses at roadside…beyond the deer checkpoint at Northville—in search of Newkirks Mills, Scotch Bush, Irish Settlement…and the settlements of others along the southern edge of the Park? Small, elusive places to be sure. Places not on many maps—yet home to some. Besides, this is hunting season. While others seek buck, I hunt settlements.

Rockwood was easy to find. It's the dip in Route 29 a short distance west of Gloversville. Rockwood has seen better days. The general store is vacant. So are several houses. Even the building with the TOWN HALL sign is boarded. Apparently, the Town of Ephratah has moved its offices. All is quiet.

Then the fire siren sounded and Rockwood suddenly is alive with flashing lights speeding past Pilgrim Holiness Church and down the freshly sanded road toward Rockwood Lake. The fire department is the liveliest thing about some places. Not much goes on between fires and fairs.

Shortly beyond Caroga Creek, a trail marker pointed to Glasgow Mills, 1.25 miles down a narrow unplowed road. This time of year, Glasgow Mills is best visited by snowmobile.

246

The last home of Nick Stoner, soldier of the Revolution and War of 1812, is at Newkirks Mills. A FOR SALE sign is in front. So is an historical marker reporting Nick died here in 1855 at age 92.

Nearby, two people tried jump-starting an old Ford.

"OK...hit the switch," said the man under the hood. Without warning, the car lunged forward slightly.

"Sorry 'bout that," said the younger man behind the wheel, shifting to neutral. Suddenly the cold engine caught, belching a large, black cloud.

"Boy...that felt good," chuckled the driver.

His helper laughed, too, as he watched bald tires spin ashes onto the porch. The excitement was enough to start the neighborhood dogs howling. Sometimes Newkirks Mills doesn't need a siren.

Unfortunately, the map had misplaced the location of Scotch Bush at the end of a dead-end road. Maybe Scotch Bush is on Church Road? Sure enough, the Scotch Bush Free Methodist Church was here—its bulletin board announcing a revival meeting later in the month, and Thanksgiving Dinner, too.

Is Dempster Corners the name given to the intersection of Route 119 and English Road? There's no marker. Just a field and a house up the road where some hunters are walking.

Irish Settlement does have a road sign, but little else. There's also a sign for the Stratford Beagle Club, and a building called Crystal Lake Lodge. But the road beyond is narrow, unsanded, unplowed. It would take a snowmobile to find Irish Settlement today, at least from this side. The same can be said for Stewart Landing. Many of these roads have only a snowmobile symbol, trail marker—or nothing.

Without half trying, I found myself on an untravelled road in search of Phipps Corners. You're allowed one mistake on an unplowed back road. My mistake was not recognizing a seasonal use shortcut until I was well committed. Surprisingly, the car held to the narrow path as it slipped across the ever-changing grade, avoiding both ditch and ravine— either of which would have left me somewhat short of Phipps Corners until spring.

Finally an intersection! Never was a destination more welcome. So what if Phipps Corners had only a house or two? This was civilization. See the man walking back from the mailbox? See the car down the road? From now on, it's plowed roads or nothing.

RE-ELECT BUDD CLAUS said the hand-lettered sign on the fence in Lotville. Guess if you live here you already know what office Budd's going after. I didn't stick around to ask. The barking dogs weren't very friendly. Besides, just about everyone who runs for reelection wins.

A school bus filled with children pulled onto the road from Beaversprite Sanctuary. Now the beavers will have Middle Sprite Creek to themselves again. Nearby, smoke curls from the chimney of the modest home where Dorothy Richards, the beaver lady, once lived. Upstream, a fresh snow outlines the branches of a lodge where her animal friends still reside.

The road to Emmonsburg has a few houses, several cars, and a hunter who stiffly leans against a tree with gun at his side. Further along is a sawmill and a farm with sheep and a few cows. You know you're at the edge of the Park when you spot an operating farm.

"Don't try the road to Knappville," the conservation officer said. "It's not plowed, and nothing's up there anyway."

I took his advice, stopping instead at the roadhouse for a sandwich—and talk of the Big Buck Contest.

"How about the biggest doe?" kidded one.

"A buck's a buck," quipped his companion. "But a doe…that could be several hundred bucks. Maybe a thousand." "Depending on the judge…huh?"

Already the Big Buck Contest poster is filled with entries. Looks like the hunters of deer have been doing better than this hunter of settlements. At least today.

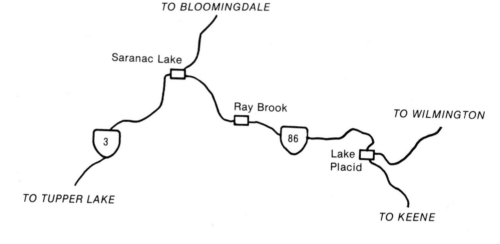

TO BLOOMINGDALE

Saranac Lake

Ray Brook

TO WILMINGTON

3

86

Lake
Placid

TO TUPPER LAKE

TO KEENE

**SARANAC LAKE,
RAY BROOK,
LAKE PLACID**

THIS December day is more twilight than daylight. Soon, gray skies swallow gray hills as snow swirls earthward, and winter spins its bleak cocoon over the Adirondack landscape.

Still, Radio Saranac is upbeat: "There's good weather news and bad weather news," joked the announcer. "Forget the bad. You're looking at it. But guess what? It's going to clear, and the sun'll come out. Not tomorrow—but today!"

Annie couldn't have sung a brighter forecast. So Radio Saranac stays on. So do the car lights as you follow the state truck spreading sand, listening to the Christmas chatter from Radio Shack—of VCRs, cordless phones, computers. A far cry from the days consumer electronics meant a high-rise radio in the living room.

What is it about this Holiday that brings back memories of childhood? Like only yesterday you see the little Christmas tree which sparkled through the frosted window at the Corner Drug Store. Must have been real frost, too—nothing from an aerosol can in those days. Surely you remember the electric train going around and around the Whitman chocolates, the Parker pen and pencil sets—all the Rexall products? How commercial! But young eyes see things differently—especially where there's an electric train. That was about the prettiest sight ever!

Now…driving along Main Street you wonder: Will the kids window-gazing at this year's Christmas hold special a snowy day they came to Saranac Lake to shop a little, and look a lot? Will they remember the pretty tree at Paul Smith's Christmas Shop…or how the old man treated everyone to lunch at Lydia's, then let them stay until after dark when downtown came alive with white lights? Years from now, will they think back on this day they came to town?

251

By then Saranac Lake will be different. But that's nothing new. Things are always changing here, ever since Capt. Pliny Miller built his sawmill where the dam now stands. That was early in the nineteenth century, years before Dr. E. L. Trudeau found improved health—and a new life which transformed this remote lumbering community into a world-renowned health resort.

"These were all cure cottages along here," said the woman walking up the hill on Helen Street. "You can tell by the porches. Now they're homes or apartments. Some are rented to students at the community college."

"Guess drug therapy replaced the rest cure?" I was not sure how or when.

"There's a museum in the lobby of the Trudeau Institute. It tells the whole story."

Sure enough it did—with newspaper accounts, photos, excerpts from E. L. Trudeau's autobiography, even an x-ray of his diseased lung. These days, the Institute conducts research in immunology. Above the lobby is a display of flags representing the home countries of the visiting scientists. They come from all over the world.

Leaving the Institute, you notice a tiny house huddled in its shadow. This must be "Little Red," the first cure cottage, which was

featured on the 1934 Christmas Seal. To this day it looks the same, a large wreath adorning its door and fresh snow capping its roof. Still, you know "Little Red" is more than a Christmas ornament—more than a mascot. It symbolizes the very essence of this institution's remarkable past.

Robert Louis Stevenson once spent a winter in Saranac Lake at "a house in the eye of many winds with a view of a piece of running water." Today, snow drifts high along the verandah with "the air clear and cold, and sweet with the purity of forests." Perhaps the author was describing his own rest cure. Now, a rocking chair and other furniture of recent vintage are stored on the porch of Stevenson Cottage, and a black dog barks at the sight of a strange car turning around. The Saranac River, however, remains much as Stevenson described it—"a piece of running water" on this day, too.

Franklin and Essex Counties share operation of the only community college within the Adirondack Park. But North Country Community College is in recess for the holidays.

"I can't wait to get home, too," said a young man climbing the hill to the gym.

"Where's home?" I asked, thinking of some far-off place.

"I'll be in Tupper by supper," he answered with a wide grin.

These days Hotel Saranac is a "hands-on" classroom for students of the hotel management program at Paul Smith's College. The hotel's rooftop offers a view of the community and surrounding countryside.

"Always enjoy coming up here," said the student manager who showed us the way.

Below, a mosaic of streets, buildings and activities unfolded. A procession of cars slowly made its way down Main Street and out Bloomingdale Avenue. That's where the American Management Association conference center is located, at the former sanitorium. You see Church Street where the laboratory and cure facility were located, and Riverside Park where the ice castle for the winter carnival will be built next month. Directly below, a little dog traces paws and nose across fresh snow, a woman slushes across the street to the library, shoppers march to the quickness of the season. You can see why Saranac Lake is sometimes called a little city.

"It's a great view at night," said our guide. "You should come back to see the lights."

"Not a bad sight right now," I answered, looking past streets and buildings, beyond Lake Flower—toward wilderness mountains touching the snow clouds of December.

Unless you're looking for the road marker, Ray Brook passes

254

without notice. Saranac Lake and Lake Placid nudge this prime commercial strip on either side. Still, Ray Brook is not cramped for space. Gift shops, motels and other businesses maintain a respectable distance. The headquarters of the Adirondack Park Agency is here. So are offices for the State Department of Environmental Conservation. Ray Brook is on its best behavior.

Sure enough the sun appeared, exactly as Radio Saranac predicted. Not a moment too soon for the Vermont truck driver who had been spinning wheels in the Artic Cone parking lot. Now the eighteen-wheeler found traction and eased onto the highway.

Have you ever tried pinpointing a place in the Adirondacks to an out-of-stater? It's not easy. For years, I've wrestled with this problem—especially in Boston. Pittsfield is at the edge of their world. Venture beyond and you drop into a black hole.

Whenever someone from Boston asked where I lived, my standard reply was: "Just west of Pittsfield," knowing full well this was the outer limit. Their reaction was invariably the same: rolling eyes and silence …an occasional "Ohhhh…."

Tiring of this, I once answered: "It's near Lake Placid." Much to my surprise, eyes did not roll.

"But of course," came the ready reply. The Grey Poupon man

couldn't have said it better, or with more conviction.

Suddenly I had discovered the power of Lake Placid! Not that many people from Boston have actually ventured to this nether-nether land. Not that many actually knew its location. But thanks to TV and the Olympics, they had heard of it.

The magic of Lake Placid's name even extends to California, I later discovered. California, however, is in another galaxy. Best not to stretch one's luck with mention of the Adirondacks there. New York's mountains don't compute in California.

No doubt, the Olympics have forever changed Lake Placid. In 1932, however, the Winter Olympics were still simple games—played in days of innocence and hard times. Nationalism would not rear its head until the Summer Olympics came to Berlin four years later. At home, the Great Depression occupied minds and radios. America was more tuned to fireside chats than bobsled runs. To be sure, neighborhood theaters would highlight Olympic action—a few moments on Movietone News weeks after an event had passed. Movietone History, it might well have been called.

By 1980, nearly everything had changed. People had money, living rooms had TVs, and the Olympics had a ready audience of millions. This was a whole new game, for advertisers as well as players. For participating countries, too—as several now used the Olympics to make a political statement. Quickly, Lake Placid was thrust into prominence beyond expectation.

Lake Placid no doubt was the smallest place ever to host the games, a fact duly noted by network reporters. Time and again Lake Placid was called "a tiny mountain hamlet." But to Adirondack eyes, the community assumes a different dimension. Over ten percent of all people in this six-million acre Park live within a few miles of Olympic Arena.

Somehow Lake Placid retains its old-country charm despite new development spawned by the Olympics. The view of lake and mountains remains unspoiled. Shops, restaurants, hotels and inns work overtime to maintain the glamour. So do the visitors strolling Main Street in the fashionable image of skiers. Not everyone thus attired makes it to the slopes of Whiteface.

Lake Placid's children take the village's high profile in stride. Their school is just across the street from Olympic Arena where the marquee announces an upcoming hockey game between the U.S.A. and Russia. The kids race for freedom as their school day ends—and fun time starts.

"Going to the game?" a boy asked his friend.

"Naw...can't be as good as the Olympics."

"How would you know? You were just a kid then."

Behind them, two girls walked slowly along, heads down. They were engaged in serious conversation.

"Are you mad?" asked one.

"What I told you was personal. I didn't expect half the school to know."

"I'm sorry."

Soon they joined the other kids snowballing, giggling, and shouting down from the Olympic flags to their friends in the skating oval. All was forgiven.

Mirror Lake Inn is decorated in its holiday finery. Never had it looked better—and never again would it look quite the same—for this renowned inn was to be hit by fire a few weeks later. Remarkably, service remained uninterrupted while the inn was rebuilt and dining room murals restored by Averil Conwell, the original artist, who performed this demanding task at age 94. By summer, the reimaging of Mirror Lake Inn was complete.

Lake Placid is ever in transition. Condominiums are under construction on Lake Road. The landmark Lake Placid Club is in the process of conversion, too. But even Melvil Dewey, its founder and originator of the Dewey Decimal System, would be hard pressed to classify the Club's

present status. Plans for its future are ever-changing.

At the Olympic ski jump facility, the young athletes shuffle across the parking lot after practice. Day after week after month they train—hoping for a brief moment of Olympic glory. Practice may be a grind, but today it ended with a grin for one young jumper. Dancing across the slippery lot to the beat from his Walkman earmuffs, his feet suddenly flew up...and down he went.

"Guess that's my best jump of the day!" he exclaimed with a big smile.

An old building is about to be moved from Old Military Road, a sign attached to its exposed framing announcing: "I've been here 112 years—time to move on." But where will this building go? To some overgrown field so snow and ice might soon bring it to earth? Or will it find a new foundation and porch, a fresh coat of paint—and another century of usefulness?

And what about the people who chose to live in this expanse of mountains, lakes, woods? Is it time for them to move on as well? Some contend the bear and deer, the little birds and animals are the only natives—that Man has always been a visitor. Is this to be a farewell tour of the little places—the "last hurrah" to a life of independence on the edge of wilderness? The final chapter is yet to be written.

At journey's end, you arrive at the mountain farmstead of abolitionist John Brown. Dusk drops its curtain across the Plain of Abraham as the statue of man and child fades from view...

Night claims the woods

but above the plain

faint daylight lingers.

For this moment

meadow and mountain,

man and child

are one—

twilight's truth

transcending darkness.

260

INDEX

262

264

266